PARENTING WITH PURPOSE
"SHINE"

PARENTING Shine WITH PURPOSE

Discovering and Developing
the Hidden Talent and Leader Within Your Child.
Ages 0-18

But we have this treasure in earthen vessels, that the
excellency of the power may be of God, and not of us.
II Corinthians 4:7

Glenda Andrus

CLASSIC
PUBLISHING
Dover, Delaware

Parenting With Purpose "Shine"
By Glenda Andrus

Copyright ©2005 by Glenda Andrus

ISBN 0-974741418

Unless otherwise indicated, all scripture quotations are
taken from the *King James Version* of the Bible.

Illustrations by Shiloh Andrus
Cover and layout design by Angela Andrus

Published by
Classic Publishing
256 Blue Heron Road
Dover, Delaware 19904

To order additional copies or other publications by Glenda Andrus,
please contact Pocket Full O' Stars Inc. 302-424-4652

DEDICATION

This book is affectionately dedicated to my mother,
Ollie W. Brock,
the most beautiful lady in the world.
Thank you for instilling Godly love into all of your children.
God painted the horizon with stars and you told me I could reach them.
My childish hands were too small and my heart could not understand,
then you lifted me. With your gentle brush of love and prayers,
my heart soars to the stars of faith where all things are possible.

Affectionately to my mother-in-law,
Bethel Andrus,
the loveliest lady I know. Your hands and heart molded the
little boy who would one day become my love, my husband.
May you know you are honored and treasured forever in my heart.

THEIR MEMORY LIVES FOREVER
IN OUR HEARTS

My dad, Rev. G. W. Brock
My father-in-law, Leon R. Andrus
This book would not exist without your love and example.
So many times your inspiration has given me the desire to achieve.
May you know I simply love you forever.

CONTENTS

Foreword by Janet Trout

It has been said, "Kids come with no guarantee or instruction manual." Well, Glenda has changed that! The guarantee part still applies but the risk will definitely be reduced when you use this "instruction manual."

Relationships is one of the buzzwords used everywhere today. A great deal of the current social ills is being attributed to relationships that have gone sour or that are non-existent. The most tragic scenario is played out as people raise their children without preparation and an understanding of the process. Many are doing so without any kind of instruction.

Excited about the arrival of a new baby, most parents have no clue about what to do—from the beginning—to build a strong relationship with their children. Part of the problem in Christian circles is the lack of literature. Glenda has changed that, too.

For the Christian, a strong relationship begins—and ends—with God. A healthy relationship with one's child arises out of faith, and a sense of the call one feels to be a parent. In that faith, and with ample instruction, parents are able to accomplish far more than they ever imagined possible.

A person can become a parent simply by having a baby. But, far too few understand how the process should be played out. When the kids turn out right, life is good. But, too often, we unknowingly damage children and live out strained relationships and broken lives. In the midst of that tragedy, the most important relationship is ignored—our spiritual connection with God.

In *Parenting with Purpose*, Glenda has captured a few stars herself! Now, she has cast them before all who want to "follow the Star" to discover and develop the talents in their children. This manual will inspire, instruct, encourage, and challenge parents who need practical tools in the process of parenting.

Understanding the Layout

Parenting is the hardest job we will ever have. Yet, it is the most important one. *Parenting With Purpose, "Shine"* presents an instructional adventure to help bring out the best in parents and children. This study offers information for ages 0-18 years old and is laid out in a context that can be used by parents or easily adapted for teachers. Discover the five secrets of unwrapping the "Shine" within your child; a featured section unique to this book. When you apply these techniques, you will find your child's "Shine" and bring out the best in his or her talents, temperaments, learning styles, and leadership skills. The material is laid out in seven chapters packed with ideas and stories using stars and kites as mascots. Each chapter concludes with an evaluation for quick review. Enjoy finding your quality parenting skills while having fun loading your *Pockets Full O' Stars* and bringing home the "Shine."

Phase I – Analyze
Phase II – Strategize
Phase III – Personalize

In Phase I – Analyze (Chapters 1-2)
·   Encouraging Seeing the Big Picture
·   Setting Priorities
·   Encouraging Goal Setting

In Phase II – Strategize (Chapters 2-6)
·   Building Relationships
·   Identifying Communication and Parenting Styles
·   Fostering Strong Family Characteristics
·   Discovering and Developing Talent and Leadership
·   Respectful Disciplining, Hedges, Dating Guidelines
·   Discussing Hard-To-Talk-About Issues

In Phase III – Personalize (Chapter 7)
·   Evaluating for Parenting with Purpose
·   Mapping Your Personal Parenting Profile

INTRODUCTION

Parenting With Purpose

Trying to find our way in parenting sometimes reminds me of wiping a steamed mirror in a closed bathroom. Have you ever been there? Each time you rub the steamed mirror to clear it, more fog appears, leaving you no option but to find a door to open for fresh air. It is the same in parenting. Just as you get through one stage... the fog from the next one comes rushing in. You get them through the feedings, past the diaper stage, and just when you think the fog has at last lifted, the tyranny of the twos settles in. Seasons and stages of life happen to all of us. I am no longer only a mom, I am a Nana; and believe me, it's a brand new experience. I am starting all over in my journey of high hopes and looking for a manual. May this book serve as a door, opening your life to a fresh, new awareness of our parenting purpose.

Living the best life is one that is filled with purpose. Sometimes parents ask, "How do you keep in touch with the main purpose, when just the mundane leaves you depleted and running on empty?" Even with the jet-age conveniences of today, keeping life's purpose in focus seems more challenging than ever. With all the different roles and clamor around us, it is very easy just to live in a parenting survival mode and have a fuzzy idea of the purpose of it all. To understand our purpose as parents, we really must keep a grip on words such as God, value, goals, and time. As you journey through this book, may your horizons expand and your purpose rise as you soar above the clouds of mediocrity and fill your Pockets Full 'O Stars of *PARENTING WITH PURPOSE* and "Shine."

Mission Statement

It is my belief that every child can shine in some area. I believe children are gifts from God, and they are the heart of our future. We are all individuals and have different temperaments, varying shapes, sizes, and colors; but, in the heart of each one of us lies a dream like a small flicker... to become. Unless someone discovers the flame and fans it, in time it will be snuffed out by the despair all around. If we can find the flame of each child, soon enough, it will rise and shine like a star giving warmth and glow all around. I believe that each human has the capacity to become. This manual offers five secret techniques to discover each child by unwrapping his "Shine." This, in essence, is finding his hidden talents which are the keys that unlock his self-worth where his leadership traits emerge. My passion is to offer a plan of hope and a ray of light in the darkness of life's situations... so parents and children can emerge like rising stars and bring the light home and shine.

Mission Purpose

I believe that each human being has a purpose designed by God, the Creator of life. I believe the closer one comes to the divine purpose of their life, the more fulfilled they become. As parents, we become the steward of the lives entrusted into our hands. My passion is to offer a plan of hope and a ray of light in the dark room of life, so parents can refocus on their purpose and bring out the best in their child... and "Shine."

NOTE FROM THE AUTHOR

I always found it more interesting if I felt I knew a little about the one who wrote the book. As you open your heart with me in this book, may you know it was written in hopes of helping other parents like myself, seeking answers, not as one who feels they have mastered the art. Thank you for journeying with me. I will try to sum up 34 years in a happy nut-shell.

You see, my husband, Royce, and I know what it is like to stay up for feedings. I remember one night being so sleepy after one of these feedings we fell back to sleep only to awaken coughing from the smoke of burning bottle nipples. We know what it is like getting ready for church with three girls and one son, looking for tiny shoes, socks, ribbons, and finally giving up and going to church with the baby in only one shoe. I was always sure this was a test when I would return and find the shoe staring at me in a most obvious place. What memories!

We know what it is like to see all the funny little faces they can make and hear a zillion questions come when you are most worn out. I'll never forget when Joel was around two years old, during his bedtime prayers, I always said, "Jesus is with you." One night, to my surprise, Joel answered back in his two year old way, "Uh uh. He downstairs." Joel had a large stuffed soldier that my brother, Terry, had given him which we normally placed over his bed. I didn't realize it, but each night as I prayed, Joel thought the toy soilder was Jesus, until this night. He had played with this particular toy and we had forgotton to bring it back upstairs. We still laugh as we remember Joel saying, "Uh uh. He downstairs."

I knew what it was like to be like David on the hills, taking care of my little sheep when no one was around. I fought off bears of fear and lions of doubt as well as loneliness. My children have become our closest friends. We knew what it was like to travel nearly 1,800 miles each year for 28 years to see grandparents and precious family to give our children roots. Would you believe after 28 years God blessed us like Joseph and now my mother, my two sisters, and their families have found their home in the East.

We knew what it was like to give our children love from a home-missionaries point of view. But there was always a loving hand somewhere close by and always God made us aware of how much He loved them.

We've suffered with our children through loss; and even walked through the valley of death losing precious friends, our hearts wrenching in grief, watching them sing a song of praise while their hearts were on the floor. We have felt the sting of death, losing both our dads and our children's grandfathers. We have sung the song of Job in the night, "The Lord giveth and the Lord taketh, blessed be His holy name."

We also now know the unspeakable joy of celebrating life. Our daughter and son-in-law, who according to medical reasons were not to give birth, have brought us two handsome grandsons. Thankfully, the times of celebration have been more than the grief, as our hearts have sailed through college and high-school graduations, academic accomplishments, and other uplifting shining events. Most of all, I am thankful for the opportunity to see our children grow in love and service to our Lord Jesus.

Children With Special Needs

I would like to extend a word of thanks and praise to the parents of children with special needs. Among these parents are many of my own dearest friends and family. The list could go on and on from the precious children who struggle physically to those who are mentally challenged. Parents, you are worthy of accolades of honor for the love and care you give to your children. While this manual cannot address each specific need at length, (a book in itself), it is important to note and be thankful for the advanced knowledge one might gain from professional help and support services available in your area. My prayers and love go to you as you constantly seek the best for your families.

Most families sooner or later experience a challenge of their own. My own family faced their challenge as my mother held me in her arms - a daughter who would have a severe complex curvature of the spine, scoliosis. What blessed parents I had. With all the challenges of scoliosis, they never gave up hope but, instead became my front row encouragers. How can I thank them enough for all they did for me?

Today, I write to you with gratefulness of heart, for God has given my husband, Royce, and I the blessing of four wonderful children. To them, I also dedicate this book. May you be blessed as you choose *Parenting with Purpose*.

Understanding the Needs of the Family:

The family is the fundamental of society's institutions, for it is within the family setting that character, morality, a sense of responsibility, and wisdom are best nurtured in children. This is not new, yet in America today, the family institution is being steadily dismantled, even held in disdain by many leaders in the political, academic, and media elite (Fagan, Heritage Foundation).

WHY STARS AND KITES?

My Life On Hold

It was another freezing northeastern winter. What was I, a southern girl, doing in Milford, Delaware, anyway? These questions filled my mind as I desperately tried to find my way. I heard the door close as my husband went to church and left me behind. But, at the moment, everything was put on hold. I was suffering from rheumatoid arthritis. I could not move even one muscle in my fingers without torturous pain. In my despair, I began to think life was over for me, and I was only 28 years old. My mind raced back to my childhood when I was faced with a severe, complex curvature of the spine. How thankful I am to God for parents, a physician, and most of all His touch that helped me walk again and stand "normal." With college and marriage behind me, I was now faced with the challenges of "real life." I was excited to begin teaching, yet still trying to find my place beside my husband's calling. Now, it was all a blur. I began to think God did not even care or know that I existed.

The Miracle Moment

When Royce left that cold day and the door closed behind him, it jarred my entire being. What a deficit I was. Being alone, I reached for a book near my bed that a mentor and college principal, Rev. Fred Foster, had left us. Struggling with my emotions, I finished reading the book entitled, *The Gift of Agabar,* by Og Mandino, an allegory of a little boy who brought down stars with his kite to keep himself and his sister alive. This book was fantastic, but I was still left struggling. Exasperated, I prayed and asked God to speak to me through someone; just to let me know He knew I existed and that He cared. He did! The miracle moment occured through a dream that changed the rest of my life. Suddenly, my phone rang. It was my sister, Ann. She said, "Glenda, I had a dream! My son Darlwyn said, "Mother, teach me how to fly a kite." I said, "Darlwyn, you have the kite. What you need is the string."

God let me know it was not just a coincidence - a dream, a boy, and a kite! My life was transformed! To think, God had my address and phone number. Shortly after this incident, I received my healing. Since then, stars, kites, and strings have been my inspiration. God let me know that I had the kite, the vehicle into the heavens, but what I needed was the string of faith. Heavenly promises are His stars that we can catch with our kite and string of faith; they are the only way we can reach into the heavens. Yet, so many times we try on our own to reach the things of God. We can all reach into the sky for things money will never purchase. God's treasure chest is as vast as the horizon.

To you, my dear friends, may you never give up, no matter how bleak the situation might look. In fact, just for a moment, step outside your window. The horizons are wrapped with stars of God's love. May stars of love, joy, and peace light your life as you fly into God's heavenly treasures.

CHAPTER SYMBOLS

Star Talk

Mascot and Guide
(I will help you find star value in each lesson.)

Kite Talk
What can I do to have winning kids? What kind of fabric do I
need to relate to the harsh winds? How far can I fly? What strings do I pull? How
long can I fly? As we put our kites together through the fabric, sticks, and attachments, we will discover what kind of stuff we are made of for raising kites and kids.
To study our kite-flying skills, we will start with the fabric of our kite and continue
from there. See you next when you choose your fabric for kites.

"High Hopes Hill"
Stands for the Journey of Parenting.

Kite Kit Toolbox:
Vocabulary Toolbox

Each Tool Box will contain important
vocabulary from the chapter.

*"When mothers and fathers belong to each other and strive to belong to God in wor-
ship the greatest strengths emerge and the least problems are present."*
Patrick Fagan, The Heritage Foundation

Shine

SHINE: Personal Mapping, Parenting Shine Chart, and Parenting Promises Featuring "Heaven's Art Gallery"

Kite Flying Tips: Endurance, (Stress and Anger Management) Lifestyles, and Envisioning Stars

Star Dust Prince and Princess in Training: Etiquette, Dating, and Hard-to-Discuss Issues

Raising Kites and Kids: Disciplining Techniques, "Shine" Disciplining Plan, Parenting Styles

Abilities, "Using the Shine Plan": Leadership, Academics, Talents, and Time

Together, Building Relationships: ABC's: Attaching, Bonding, and Communicating

Seeing the Big Picture: Choosing Core Values

About the Book:
Climbing High Hopes Hill

What big dreams, like stars, lie on the bottom of your heart's floor? Do you have big plans for your child, but keep bumping your head on the daily grind? Just getting them out the door leaves you exhausted and late. We know the stars are up there. God put them all around us. But how can we reach them in a world where we are taught that the first one in line gets the prize? Are you tired of being the referee, and the kids using you for a taxi and making you late? How will they make it to college when they can't remember their lunch box? Then, the other side of the coin is you. You need help. Even now, as you read this book, you really feel you don't have the time. You still would like to pull down a couple of stars for yourself, but somehow you still keep falling through the cracks of life. Are you tired of trying to pull all those important strings to find that someone else got there first, or hearing "Sorry, you don't qualify" or "You over qualify?" We are either too poor, too rich, or too late. Good news! Forget the dysfunctional labels. With God there are no accidents. You are somebody, and "your" child can "Shine!"

Shine

Reaching for a way to turn on the motor inside the child, our team came up with an action plan I called "Shine." With a team and staff working together, it has been our delight to see the benefits of offering a stage for students and parents to celebrate their lives at Lighthouse Christian Center, Milford, Delaware, bringing out the confidence and the shine. In the next few pages, it is my desire to take you on an upward journey of building your child's profile, learning his personality traits, discovering the way he learns best, and finding his hidden talents and leadership character.

In this book we offer nuggets for finding hidden talent and a plan for teaching character, learning styles, and building in our child's profile some outstanding "Shine." The "Shine" plan we developed was enacted and proven by local, award-winning children participating in national level events. That's not all; we have not left you out. As a parent, we want you to shine, too. That is why we developed a simple evaluation plan, a tool to bring out your best, so you can gather your pocket full of stars and shine.

I fully believe you can emerge from life's baggage, laundry, and kid driving to become a kite flyer and shine.   There are rules of the game you must follow, but everyone can bring home the shine. With the help of kites and stars illustrations, I want to offer you a way up. Kite flyers cross culture, race, and other background baggage to shine. How high do you want to go? How much string is in your pocket? Good parents keep their hands on the string and fly the kite. Kites cannot fly on the ground...our first stop is High Hopes Hill where we check our journey's destination.

...Happy Flyin' Shine! By the way, did you notice the cable for the incline lift is out of order? There are no short cuts; life is a process... so ...our first chapter begins with your climb and your assignment.

You have the desire to make it, or you would not be reading this today... and the journey of a thousand miles always starts with the first step... you're on your way!

Seeing the Big Picture
Choosing Core Values

Chapter 1

SEEING THE BIG PICTURE
CHOOSING CORE VALUES

Parent Reading About Kites and Kids

You are probably asking what does flying kites have to do with raising children? Chapter 1 teaches how good parenting is like kite flying. Both activities require a certain amount of firmness – good parenting requires solid values that give lives purpose, and good kite flying requires a firm hand and solid footing.   It is my hope that through practicing the principles in this manual, you become so adept at kite flying (good parenting) that you fly so high that you can catch the stars and hold them in your hand. Are you ready for the adventure?

"To Catch a Star and Hold it in Your Hand"

Long ago, in the year of 1897, Marie and Pierre Curie reached into a drawer where a rock had been locked; and to their amazement, it had left an imprint. It was as though a star was locked in the rock. Because of the rock's internal flame in the darkness of the drawer, an imprint of the object that had lain upon it was formed. Madam Marie Curie said of the unusual rock, "It was as though I held a star in my hand."

After years of hard labor, the Curies unlocked the rock's secret and discovered radium. Their labor on an unusual rock led to the life-saving discoveries of x-ray and radiation and altered the course of medical science forever.

May I present to you that our children are similarly locked in the drawer of our care. In the dark room called life, children are laid into our hands, and much like the x-ray process, the possibilities of imprinting on their lives are unlimited. But also like radium, if handled incorrectly, it has the power to destroy life. The power of parents and radium alike is unlimited. Good parenting has the power to change the fate of humanity. Conversely, poor parenting has the power to do irreparable damage. To turn the rock into something worthwhile is a painstaking and unrelenting job.

3

Could it be that when we enter our prayer closet, the light of God's presence fills our lives and as we submit our needs and children to Him, the most powerful Rock of all imprints His character of goodness upon them?

In a sense, children are like the star locked up inside a rock. If we nurture them persistently and continually, one day the good will shine forth. The years of painstaking nurturing will pay off. They will be of great value to mankind, perhaps even changing the direction of history for generations to come. Then, as parents, you can join Madam Curie in saying you have held a star in your hand.

The most important imprint a parent can make upon their child's life is the imprint of eternal things. Therefore, this Parenting Course bases its principles completely on the Rock of all Rocks -- Jesus Christ.

II Corinthians 4:7 -- But we have this treasure in earthen vessels, that the excellency of the power may be of God, and not of us.

The above story gives me hope for the future. Could it be that when we enter our prayer closet, the light of God's presence fills our lives and as we submit our needs and children to Him, the most powerful Rock of all imprints His character of goodness upon them? I believe prayer is the source of peace and the real point of power for purpose. He who abides in the secret place of God, dwells in the shadow of the almighty (Psalms 91:1). There, in the secret place, we find the peace and strength as parents to make it through the maze of life.

Even with all the conveniences of this day, keeping life's purpose in focus seems more challenging than ever. Supermarkets, micro-waves, central-air and heat, super heroes, videos, DVD's, and TV's in most kid's bedrooms, to name a few, have all appeared in my generation.

I chuckle when I remember a statement my grandson, Gregory, (who was three at the time) made when his dad asked him about creation. On the first day God said, "Let there be light and there was light." Then He made Adam and Eve and then God said, "Let there be toys." It's amazing the apparent truth of this generation coming from the lips of this child.

Yet, when I think back to some of my most cherished childhood memories, they didn't have anything to do with the latest gimmick. The smell of frying bacon drifting through the chilly morning air can still send my mind back to little girlhood days. I had a wise and caring mother who braved the teeth chattering early mornings to send out smells that not only awoke me as a little girl, but still arouse my emotions. Growing up in the fifties and sixties in Bogalusa, Louisiana, one picture especially stands out among the myriad of miracles my mother seemed to perform.

4

How did she manage to cook a full breakfast (eggs, bacon, grits, and always those delicious biscuits) and have our clothes ready, even socks, and get us out the door by 7:10? By the way, our clothes were mostly cotton and needed ironing, to say nothing of the sewing that she did. You see, there was quite a number of us kids getting ready for school by the one-room heater. There were eight children altogether, but spaced out enough that only five were getting ready for school at a time, seven girls, and the family's pride and joy, a boy. I remember with childhood nostalgia, all of us hovering near the heater to dress, leaving a huge stack of clothes for mother to stow away and start all over again the next day.

Yet, do you know what I remember more than the warmth from the little heater? It is the greater warmth of the love that surrounded that room. It has been over fifty years ago now, but I still recall those beautiful brown eyes as they twinkled with sheer delight, and those priceless soft hugs that assured me I was loved beyond measure. When the yellow school bus stopped in front of our house, our pockets bulged with stars of meaning. Was it because of monetary wealth? No. It was because someone kept life's purpose intact.

When any of us look back to the memories we hold dear, they are usually not made up of those things that come in tangible values. I am not suggesting that we need to go back to the one-room heater to find life's purpose. But how can you grab purpose by the neck and say, "Ah, I have found you, and now I am going to keep you." Where is the menace that keeps us running like a lost train on a never-ending, meaningless track? Has society, like a vacuum cleaner, pulled us into a vicious mental pressure cycle that says, "Taking care of our children is not the cool thing." It is as though we have been told that the working women, with their careers in place, are the real pace-setters, and the rest of us are pitifully wasting our time changing diapers and dutifully taking up space and time.

I want to encourage each mother and father raising children in this pressured society. No one is perfect, and keeping your values as priority is a constant job. I seriously do not know how a mother could physically do all that one did in years gone by. What about the pressure fathers face in balancing the work day with family life and being the Mr. Everything for everybody? His pressure is no less; however, if we remove the pressure of what society is expecting, we can see time spent with family is one of the most important jobs of all. It is truly a call to battle in the front lines for saving our families and, like Esther, even saving our nation.

Tim Elmore gives an interesting picture chart showing the effects society has had upon America. This chart shows the decline of homes simultaneously with the decline in God and respect for authority. This chart makes clear that when life values like respect for authority and purpose decline, so do homes.

Trends showing Degeneration of Homes in American Society

Era of Time	Names	Attitude to God & Authority	Purpose
1900-1928	Victorian	Respectful	To earn enough for living.. and wished they had more education to get a better job
1930-1945	Depression Survivors	Endure Them	Taught children to seek education … to earn enough … to get education first
1946-1964	Boomers	Replace Them	Education first: Godless
1965-1983	Groovers, Hippies-Yippies	Ignore Them	Decline of Homes
1984-2001	Millennials	Choose Them	Job first: Home's degeneration

Chart idea taken from Tim Elmore, *Nurturing the Leader within Your Child* (77).

Matching Priorities and My Time

Two years ago, the paramedics with all of their life support gear pulled into our neighborhood about three o'clock in the morning. Could it be someone in my own neighborhood was facing an emergency? A nearby nurse friend was called. Someone's life was shutting down; their blood pressure was reading 40/30 with a declining oxygen level of 30. Astonishing as this may sound, that someone was me. As I was fading away, my priorities quickly lined up. Was I ready to meet God? I did not want to leave my husband, Royce, and my children. I have one married daughter, Cherie, and her husband, Greg, who live next door with my grandchildren, Gregory (4) and Garrison (1). Upstairs, my other three children were awakened to the trauma… Shiloh, Angela, and Joel. It was too early to awaken my mother, sisters, or brother. What about the dear church family who support us in love and prayer? All was fading quickly.

I was told later that no one knew why the sudden, near loss of my life occurred. Although I may never know just what happened, I do know now, more than ever, that life can suddenly be gone without any warning. Priorities have a way of quickly lining up when life starts coming to a sudden halt. The pressure of society, prestige, and even life's accomplishments, are not a priority when life is about to end. It is amazing how many activities, even those that we think are harmless, can be changed when faced with life or death.

From my heart to yours, may we choose to keep our priorities in order every day, for we never know when our last day will be. Almost daily, this traumatic experience makes me think of what one thing I would want my loved ones to remember about me. Would they remember me for making time for them? Were my projects a priority over their relationship? These important questions have made me take serious looks at my life's priorities.

At the beginning of this book, I would like for you to join me by asking yourself these serious and important questions. This is truly for self-evaluation, and I hope it serves as a new beginning for the rest of your life as it has to mine.

Below is an opportunity for you to seriously think about what matters most in life.   The good thing is that you hold the pencil in your hand now. You have the ability to make the choice.

Choosing Our Big Picture

*What one thing would you want
said about you when you come to the end of life?*

1.
2.
3.
4.
5.

Family, Recreation, Career, Education, God

*Beginning with most important to least important, prioritize the above
words in order of value for your life.*

Does your big picture of life match your time activities?

Did you spend at least one hour interacting with family?
Yes - No
Do you spend any time in prayer?
Yes - No
Did you spend 40 hours working last week?
Yes - No
Did you spend 1 hour in your goal of education last week?
Yes - No
Did you volunteer for church work?
Yes - No
Did you laugh at least once a day?
Yes - No
Did you go to church Sunday?
Yes - No

What priorities do you need to change?

"The Hand that rocked the cradle is disappearing, what about the baby, what about the nation?" "We were born for a higher destination than the stars."

So You Want Your Child to Become a Winner...

At the McDonald's drive-through window, a voice blares through the intercom, "Would you like to try our super-size combo today or a single with extra cheese?"

Unfortunately, today's drive-through, instant-gratification culture has imprinted more than hamburgers on our brains. Somehow, this fast-lane syndrome is carrying over to all parts of our lives. When we talk about kids and family, however, we have to get past the drive-through concept and know our choices are for keeps. It's not, "If you don't like this one, drive to the next drive-through and see what's on the menu." This baby thing is for keeps. Life is not an event; life is a process where decisions have long-term consequences.

Perhaps life has forced you into the fast lane. You keep looking for an exit sign, but the beltway has none. It is like you have driven onto an asphalt conveyor belt marked "forever." You are about to holler, "Help!" when you notice a star with chubby cheeks and dimples has fallen into your lap. You inspect this bright, shining creature and wonder where the "Operating Manual" is. No matter how your starry-eyed baby came to be, you quickly realize it cannot be sent back. Returning the package is not a valid choice for those who have come to High Hopes Hill.

New parents have so many questions. What do we do now? How do we start? What can we do as parents to guarantee a safe passage through childhood that makes shining transitions into adult realities? While no guarantees come with any baby, principles exist that guarantee results and are proven to aid parents in their childrearing journey.

What is your Purpose in Life?
First of all, Select the Big Picture as a Parent:

As a parent, what big picture do you want? In other words, what goals in life do you desire for yourself and your child? Selecting the big picture has to do with God, family, and how you define life.

"A Winning Child"

Betty looked out the window at her little kindergarten daughter, and wiping a tear from her eye said, "World, please don't take the sparkle from her blue eyes and the smile from her dimpled cheeks." That plea alone will not keep our children from the streets of vandalism, lifestyles of promiscuity, or academic failure.

What is the secret of keeping the winning attitude, the sparkle and spunk of innocence, and of nurturing the good until it blossoms full term into adulthood? In his book, *The Successful Child*, Dr. William Sears (2002) says, "Parents who help children taste success in one area are usually setting them up to be winners in other areas" (73). Sears observed the following attributes common in winning children:

1. A quality that enables him to work well in a group
2. An understanding of how other people feel
3. A respect for others
4. An ability to move confidently from one skill to another
5. A built-in formula that loves to meet challenges whether it is gaining knowledge, playing sports, or other activities

If we could add a number six, the winning child would land safely into matrimony and become a responsible, productive adult.

What Kind of Home Develops a Winning Child?

Below are three possible, big-picture scenarios. Only one of them is conducive to the nurture and development of a winning child.

Story #1

When Ann Lee was 21 years old and was asked what her big picture in life was, she said, "My biggest desire is to have a loving family." However, at 35, Ann Lee had been married twice, and now her third relationship was pending. She had managed to build a fantastic career at a respectable corporation. Now, she reflects back on her big picture and asks what she did wrong. She has two children, a daughter who is 10 years old going into adolescence, and a son of 14. Her daughter spends a lot of time on the phone talking to the opposite sex. Her son spends a lot of time hanging out in the neighborhood. He has already been caught with a violent neighborhood gang a couple of times. Now Ann is starting to have guilty moments wondering where her son is and what her daughter is doing. Still, Ann continues pursuing her career and cannot figure out what went wrong with her big picture. Can you help her?

Story #2

Judy is 30 years old and the mother of three children who are 12, 7, and 5. Before marriage, Judy and Dan decided their big picture would be God first, family second, and each other third. Her husband, Dan, has to spend a lot of overtime trying to meet their financial obligations; but because they both have a big picture of family values as their priority, Dan saves each evening to have dinner and family time together with his wife and children. Although, each night the amount of time he can spend at home may vary, Judy tries to compensate by doing a little extra with the children at those times. However, over the years they have managed to keep the dinner hour and church time as priorities. Dan takes their 12-year-old son to sax lessons on Thursday night and their younger 7- year-old daughter to piano lessons. While they are away, Judy gives the five-year-old sound tracks and singing lessons. She also takes her to gymnastic classes on Tuesday. Everyone is up and going. Dan and Judy are happy, even though life gets hectic at times, because they have a deep contentment knowing that they are investing in the big picture.

Story #3

On the night Bridgett was killed, it was the child's sighing that upset her father's girlfriend, then 20 and a student (who was studying for an exam). After failed attempts to quiet the child, Davis watched as Meridian, who was not the child's mother, pushed Bridgett's forehead with her finger, picked the child up by her head and flung her toward him. Then, he and Meridian stuffed a pair of socks into Bridgett's mouth, placed a hooded sweatshirt backward around the child's head and secured it with duct tape. Bridgett then was placed in a closet and partially covered with clothes. Meanwhile, Davis and Meridian sat down to eat dinner (Fagan and Hanks, 1997, 15). Statistics show that every day 6 children die from child abuse in America (Fagan and Hanks, 1997, 1).

As a Parent, Which Picture Would You Select?

Selecting the big picture as a parent "seems" easy enough. We all want winning children. We all want them to have a happy, loving, home life and become responsible, loving, productive adults who shine. According to the Heritage Foundation report, over 60% of American children have big pictures that are confused by broken homes and broken hearts.

Never has there been such a day when lives were faced with so much pressure. As adults, we know that we should be busy taking care of our lives. We start, but get derailed by the pressure of phone calls, sickness, death, or a friend who betrays us. Living by a code of ethics can seem mundane when across the street lives the single with their weekend flings, jazzy cars, and snazzy vacation destinations.

This line of mental questioning easily comes to mind, especially when waltzing to the mailbox is your day's moment out. You get the picture, the days of our lives is truly the "Daze" of our lives; and the little white rabbit in Alice in Wonderland keeps jumping in front of us telling us we are late. Somehow, we knew that but, "Just where we are going would be the helpful thing now." Life has left us with the impression that we owe our children something. If we just knew what and where to find it.

While the above may be an overplay with words, the truth is that too many of us have no big picture. Astoundingly, those who are supposedly the goal-oriented ones find themselves in a jungle of airports, appointment books, or palm pilots. Too many times, the big picture of home is only dreams of yesterday with fading childhood memories. Demanding lifestyles are leading to ambiguous mindsets, discontentment, and despair. With individuals having so many different roles to play and so many assignments each day, unless they have clearly decided what their life's big picture is, the most important things in life may get lost in the shuffle.

Demanding lifestyles are leading to ambiguous mindsets, discontentment, and despair.

Star Talk ☆

Parents who help their child taste success in one area are actually setting them up to become winners in other areas.

Everyone wants a winning child – one who makes high marks academically, one who is socially charming, responsible, and respectful. Yet, as parents entering the new millennium, the challenge is more astonishing than ever. Statistics show that in 1950 for every 100 children born that year, 12 were born into a broken family (4 were born out of wedlock and 8 suffered the divorce of their parents). By the year 2000, that number had risen fivefold – for every 100 children born, 60 entered a broken family (33 were born out of wedlock, and 27 suffered the divorce of their parents). We must conclude that over the last 50 years America has evolved from being preponderantly "a culture of belonging" to being a "culture of rejection." In the conclusion to his study entitled "The Breakdown of the Family: The Consequences for Children and American Society", Heritage Foundation researcher, Patrick Fagan (1998) said, "When mothers and fathers belong to each other and strive to belong to God in worship, the greatest strengths emerge and the least problems are present" (22). In short, an intact family unit with God at the center is a good start toward rearing a winning child. (See graph 1 on pg. 14)

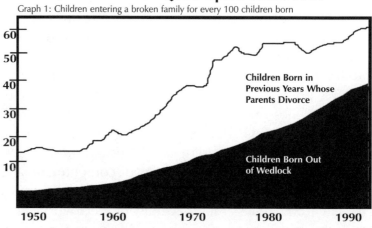

The Break Down of The Family, Patrick Fagan

What are the Basic Elements Found in a Strong Family Unit?

The family is the fundamental of society's institutions, for it is within the family setting that character, morality, responsibility, ability, and wisdom are nurtured best in children. This concept is not new; yet in America today, the family institution is being steadily dismantled, even held in disdain by many leaders of the political, academic, and media elite. These external forces exert great pressure on the fabric of family. If left unchallenged, their erosion of family and disdain for family values will have serious consequences.

However, families also face internal pressures that eat away at family unity. A family's disintegration may have its root causes in something as uninvited as a prolonged illness, a sudden death, or may be the consequences of poor choices – each of these may cause the downward spiral of the family unit. Whatever the cause, children and adults both suffer the traumatic effects. The data on the effects of the breakdown of the family illustrate where the source of strong individuals, healthy families and stable communities are most frequently to be found. These are within marriages involved in religious worship. In other words, "When mothers and fathers belong to each other and strive to belong to God in worship, the greatest strengths emerge and the least problems are present" *(Fagan, 1998, 22).*

What are the Basic Elements Found in Raising Juvenile Delinquents?

After gathering an abundance of information concerning negative outcomes, the ten rules below accurately sum up the sad findings.

1. Do not listen to your child.
2. Do not provide routines.
3. Pay no attention when they are sad.
4. Never eat a meal together.
5. From birth to age five, use a day-care or nanny so you can focus on your career.
6. Pay no attention to what they watch, hear, or who their friends are.
7. Leave them at home alone (the neighborhood makes a great hang-out for soon-to-be delinquents).
8. Never bring them to church.
9. Make sure you argue with your spouse; your point is right and the kid will soon be insecure enough to never believe you or anyone.
10. Never say, "I love you."

Below you will read the steps which usually lead to violent crime:

Five Steps to Violent Crime

The Heritage Foundation Backgrounder (Fagan, 1995, 5-6)

Step One: Parental neglect and abandonment in early home life.
- When the baby is born, his father has already abandoned the mother.
- If his parents are married, they are likely to divorce by the third year.
- He is raised in a neighborhood with a high concentration of single-parent families.
- He does not become securely attached to his mother during the critical, early years of life.

Step Two: The embryonic gang becomes a place to belong.
- He is by now both hyperactive and difficult to endure.
- His parents' supervision is inconsistent and explosive.
- He satisfies his needs by exploiting others.
- At age five or six, he hits his mother.
- In first grade, his aggressive behavior causes problems for others.
- He is socially rejected at school by normal children.
- His life is now characterized by his own aggressive behavior, his

aggressive peers, and his hostile home life.
- He searches for and finds acceptance among similarly aggressive and hostile children.

Step Three: The emergence of the gang.
- At age 11, he is well into his bad ways.
- By age 15, he will engage in criminal behavior.
- His companions are increasingly important to him for personal identity and a sense of belonging.
- The earlier he commits his first delinquent act, the longer he will lead a life of crime.
- Many, especially the girls, will run away from home; many others just drift away.

Step Four: High violence grows in his community with the growth of single parents.
- He purchases a gun, at first mainly for self-defense.
- His group increasingly uses violence for exploitation.
- The violent young men in the group get arrested more than the nonviolent criminals.
- Most of them do not get caught at all.
- The girls become involved in prostitution while he and his group join criminal gangs.

Step Five: A new child, and a new generation of criminals begins.
- His 16-year-old girlfriend is pregnant. He has no thought of marrying her: it is not done. They will stay together for a while until the shouting and hitting starts. He leaves her and does not see the baby.
- One or two of his criminal friends are real experts in their fields.
- In his neighborhood, 4% of the delinquent families commit 50% of the crime.
- In any 3-year period, only 14% of the expert career criminals get caught. They commit hundreds of serious crimes per year.
- Most of the crime he and his friends commit is in his own neighborhood which grows less and less livable as a community.

Now that you have had a chance to look at the root causes and statistics, you may be wondering about your own strengths and weaknesses. The truth is, everyone has weaknesses and obstacles they have to overcome. In his book, *The Return Of The Ragpicker*, Og Mandino (1992) stated the problems with young people are imbedded deeper than college coed dorms. The problems have their roots bound deeply into the bedrock of the home. He added, "We have made astonishing advances in medicine and science and transportation and yet we still have little or no knowledge of how to get along with our neighbors or how we must think and act in order to change our lives for the better. There has got to be a better way to live" (112). Mandino's challenge is to change – focus on relationships and home is the best place to teach children how to think and act properly.

Defining "Your" Big Picture

As parents, the big pictures of your life are the areas that you think are the most important. Thus, the big pictures in your life showcase your values and priorities. While all of us may like to embrace the elements that could cause us to be winners, we must continue in our study and evaluate if our actions truly equal what we value. According to Dr. Sears (2002), there are key elements that distinguish the values and priorities of winning families and their homes from all others.

Children are not born winners or born juvenile delinquents. Each are developed. Statistics show where moms and dads belong to each other and each to God that better outcomes are evident. (Fagan, 1995, 5-6)

The big pictures in your life showcase your values and priorities.

Star Talk ☆

How you prioritize the following aspects of your life will help you define your big picture. Circle the number that best describes the importance of the value listed beside it. Afterwards, evaluate the results to see what values you think are the most important in your life – those values will make up your big picture.

		Least Important...			...Most Important	
•	Loving Family	1	2	3	4	5
•	God	1	2	3	4	5
•	Financial	1	2	3	4	5
•	Recreation	1	2	3	4	5
•	Fun	1	2	3	4	5
•	Food	1	2	3	4	5
•	Education	1	2	3	4	5
•	Friends	1	2	3	4	5

Let's Continue On Our Journey

To help you see the big picture of what you want in life, we will use an easy tool of evaluation. We will evaluate on three levels: analyze, strategize, and personalize. This easy, three-step, evaluation tool will move you closer to the inner core of yourself. It can help you emerge out of the shuffle of your life to see your strengths and weaknesses and attain your goals for the "Big Picture" of life.

The hand that rocks the cradle is disappearing, what about the home? What about the nation?

Evaluate:

Analyze (Chapter 1)	Strategize (Chapter 2-6)	Personalize (Chapter 7)
Understand definitions in kite toolbox	**Plan to Overcome:** · Prioritizing: · What is your big picture of life? · What is your priority? · Do your **activities match your goals?**	**Application:** ·God ·Family ·Education
Looking inside? · 3 windows · Past · Present · Future	Since you have read about setting your big picture, do you think you can improve on getting your activities to match your goal?	
My personal baggage What experiences have I had that will help or hurt my parenting skills? · Education experiences? · Life experiences? · Previous hurts or helps for marriages, etc. (previous children). · Blended family.	Name three activities you need to replace with more goal-oriented ones?	Applying Star method of Solving family issues
Looking around me · Who are my influencers? · What are my other responsibilities? Health of parents, job obligations, church involvement	**Be willing to identify my parenting style:** · Name two weaknesses · Name two strengths	Charting my personal Parenting Shine Profile…
· Identifying personal strengths and weaknesses · Personal style · Communication style · Personality temperaments · Parenting style		

Kite Talk: Hang in There

Whew! If you made it through the Valley of Despair and are still reading, you are above average. You are ready for an upward current. Standing on a strong foundation, you'll be in the best possible position for good parenting "kite flying".

Star for Your Pocket

Research shows that love between a father and mother in marriage and regular worship of God are the two fundamental strengths for the home. Thus, marriage and God constitute the fundamental roots of this nation (Fagan, 1998, 22).

Evaluation Plan

We have analyzed the definitions and values of life, and now it is time to strategize. Do your daily activities equal your values and definition of home? The daily activities you engage in to accomplish your goals may all line up when you look at them on paper. Yet, unless you actually fulfill these activities, you will not reach the star of your goals. You must really look at yourself internally, externally, and psychologically. Internally, do you lack skill; or do you have unhealthy past experiences or harmful habits in your life? Externally, are there circumstances beyond your control such as illness in yourself or others, drug or alcohol problems, or abusive situations? Psychologically, have you embraced harmful habits and negative thinking patterns passed to you from others? The internal, external, and psychological baggage that you may carry around affects your decision-making style. That is why it is imperative that you honestly analyze yourself so that you can see what makes you respond or react the way you do as a parent.

Analyzing Technique

Who am I? (Internal)	What's going on around me? (External)	How do I make my decisions? (Psychological)
Parenting Skills Other Skills Experience Habits	Things I Have No Control Over Illness Relatives Other Habits	Past baggage that affects my thinking

Kite Kit Toolbox:

Vocabulary Toolbox for Chapter I

As we set our priorities, we need to make sure our definitions of values and purpose of life equate with our big picture. Another way of wording it is, "What do you stand for?" In parenting, the big picture that you desire and the total outcome has everything to do with your definition of words such as:

- God
- Parenting
- Family
- Values
- Core Values
- Purpose
- Responsibility
- Commitment
- Children
- Home
- Health
- Role

God - Supreme author, creator and designer of Life.

Word of God – God's plan for man on earth. God's instruction book of life.

Parenting – Webster defines parenting as coming from the root word "parent", which literally means been born or produced from. Parents become the care-giver of their children. It is through their provision of food, shelter, and clothing that a sense of well-being is nurtured. As infants and young children, a parent's role has more to do with the relationships, safety, feeding, changing, and sleeping routines. As the child grows, parenting becomes broader in the sense of a general manager of their health, spirit, time, talent, intellect, and relationships. Each is dependent upon the other for the healthy development of the child. In secular Greek, the word *teleios* means mature, complete, an adult, fully grown and opposed to immature and infantile. The full meaning of the word urges growth; go on to maturity. Isn't mature growth what we want for our children? Although American culture is trying to redefine parents and family, in our study, parents and family are defined as a man and woman who conceived and brought forth the baby from their own bodies, or the child who was adopted by them.

Family – The family is the most fundamental of society's institutions for it is within the family setting that character, morality, responsibility, ability, and wisdom are nurtured best in children. Marriage between a man and a woman is the unit which constitutes a family.

Value – Webster defines value as the worth of a thing. In parenting, it would mean the worth of your care of your children. Foundational values are the core beliefs on which your home is built. Because of core beliefs and values, commitments are made and lives are molded.

Responsibility – Reliable, duty, claiming ownership

Home – Where all of the above are nurtured. The place where the heart begins its journey.

Down Drafts – A down draft is the vicious, spiraling, downward suction that takes us away from our purpose and family. Watch out for the down draft!

A Poet Once Wrote

What is Home?
It is more than the kettle on the stove,
the food in the refrigerator
… it is where the heart can rest…

What is a home?
A roof to keep out the rain.
Four walls to keep out the wind,
floors to keep out the cold.

Yes, but a home is more that.
It is the laugh of a baby,
a song of a mother,
the strength of a father,
warmth of loving hearts,
light from happy eyes,
kindness, loyalty, comradeship.

Home is first church,
first school for the young ones,
Where they learn what is right,
what is good and what is kind.
Where they go for comfort when they are hurt or sick.
Where joy is shared and sorrow is eased.
Where fathers and mothers are respected and loved…
Where children are wanted…
Where the simplest food is good enough for kings,
because it is earned.
Where money is not so important as loving kindness.
Where even the teakettle sings from happiness.

That is home.
My mother and daddy gave us one.

Anonymous

Children develop better in family environments where dad, mom, and child belong to each other and all to God.

Parenting With Purpose

What is parenting? We again ask that question with a deeper look. Parenting literally means becoming the caregiver of their children. Caring refers to that which nurtures. In human beings, care is more than the care we speak of as in care of animals. This kind of care is a higher call.

Humanity needs a set of codes to live by so people can dwell together in peace. People need divine direction from "Someone" larger than themselves (a Creator) in order to live life with purpose. With no code of conduct, man becomes his own best destroyer. Scholars agree that all civilizations which have survived succeeded because of a code of order. Which code works best is debatable. However, when a person is given the choice and evidence to prove that a particular method has been found to be true, he then has the opportunity to base his decisions upon the truth he has found. The Hebrew account of one parent who found a purpose is Abraham. He is an example of one such individual who made a decision between following his culture's morals or following God's plan.

> Genesis 12:1-3, Now the LORD had said unto Abram, Get thee out of thy country, and from thy kindred, and from thy father's house, unto a land that I will shew thee: And I will make of thee a great nation, and I will bless thee, and make thy name great; and thou shalt be a blessing: And I will bless them that bless thee, and curse him that curseth thee: and in thee shall all families of the earth be blessed.

God promised Abraham that if he would obey God's command and, by faith, leave his old life that through him all of the families of the earth would be blessed. Abraham obeyed and found his big picture in the Word of God.

The Covenant of Stars

If they would have had lottery tickets, someone would have thought Abraham won the ticket marked "Children." Even Sarah laughed, according to the story. However, Abraham is called the Father of the Faithful. For it is written in his diary that his God spoke unto him, "Abraham, as the stars so shall your seed be. From you shall all of the families of the earth be blessed" (Genesis 22:7). Wow!

Well, if you are still with me, we may as well go together with Abraham up High Hopes Hill to gaze at all those stars in the sky. Do you feel the wind blowing the sand? It surely blew on Abraham. The wind gustily tore at his robe, causing it to flow as free as his spirit. He could hear the little cry in the tent and knew the promise had come. Little Isaac had been born.

Oh, maybe this is just another fairy tale to you. Perhaps sand, stars, and an old woman and an old man is a bit simplistic for this technological age. But think for the moment of the miracle and indulge in Abraham and Sarah's sheer bliss at the birth of their promised son, in a tent, on the backside of a desert. Listen, I hear her.... Sarah, that is... "Isaac, you shall grow up with a purpose, for your father heard from God. God has made him the father of many nations. You are a prince, my son, and I shall treat you as one." She smoothed his little blanket. Then Sarah closed the tent flap to keep out the desert chill. Yet, as we look up into the night sky, we see the stars have come out. A spectacular sight! Not even the desert sand can dim the vision of these stars of promise.

You may say, "Oh, this is just a love story of how a man and woman took a journey across a desert. They really didn't know where they were going (no GPS), but they kept looking for a place (sounds almost like the hippie generation), but the voice they were following led them and fulfilled His promises."

Listen to the voices from behind the canvas flap... I believe I hear Abraham saying, "Sarah? It seems like it was only yesterday... I stood out on that mountain and heard the voice of God. Oh, Sarah, it echoed across the desert that starlit night. '...Abram, get thee out of thy country, and from thy kindred, and from thy father's house, unto a land that I will shew thee: And I will make of thee a great nation, and I will bless thee, and make thy name great; and thou shalt be a blessing: And I will bless them that bless thee, and curse him that curseth thee: and in thee shall all families of the earth be blessed'" (Genesis 12:1-3).

Abraham was 100 and Sarah was 90 when God's promise finally came to past. As you trace Abraham's family tree, you will see that promise fulfilled time and time again. Through Abraham's lineage came the Savior of the world. Abraham rejected the common big picture of success for his day and sought after the big picture, God's promises, that would birth a Savior. He first sought to follow a set of principles given to him from God, and then God blessed him.

Billy Tucker is a present-day example of a young man who found purpose for his life. He was a follower of the same God as Abraham. He found his big picture in the Word of God, making the Bible his guide for life. In fact, the Biblical record promises that all the families of the earth would be blessed if they followed the same guide as Abraham, God's Word (Geneses 12:1-3).

Selecting the Big Picture Gives Purpose

A modern day story of a young man who found purpose:
BILLY TUCKER
Today, in this millennium, there are still lives destined for purpose.

Five years ago, Billy Tucker, an 18 year old, robust and vibrant young man, left the world this testimony in a sermon he preached at Lighthouse Christian Center in Milford, DE, entitled, "I Have Found the Purpose of Life." One month after giving this testimony, Billy died in an automobile accident on January 10, 2000. After his death, the tape of his testimony was aired on JOY Radio for all the broadcast audience to hear.

I listened to Billy's voice over the radio proclaiming, "I have found the purpose of living. It is to praise and magnify my God." I thought what a contrast Billy's short life had been to many of the youth of America today. Shortly after the incident of Billy's death was the tragic shootings at Columbine High School. Because of two youths whose choices had deadly consequences, horrific atrocities befell the lives of innocent high school students that day in Littleton, Colorado. There must be a better way to live, and Billy found it. Billy was a pulley to all the youth group of his church and to those who knew him. He spent his time, whether with co-workers or friends, lifting them up and talking to them about His best friend, Jesus Christ. His purpose brought peaceful consequences to the lives of those he left behind.

Abraham found purpose, and then he passed purpose on to the next generation, Isaac. Five years ago, in this millennium, Billy Tucker testified "I have found my purpose." Parents of today have to make the tough decision between living meaningless lives or living lives filled with purpose. Making the decision to live lives filled with purpose, God's purpose, and passing that purpose on to the next generation will be the most important decision parents will ever make.

Star Talk ☆

The covenant of stars is above us, and if we look closely, we can see those bright beacons of purpose beckoning us to choose the blessed life.

From you shall all the families of the earth be blessed. Follow the path Abraham followed … the quest for God as first priority in all matters of life… yields a life of blessing. (Geneses 12:1-3 and Geneses 15:1-6)

Kite Talk

It is time for you to make the choice. Let the star covenant help.
Are you parenting with purpose?

· What does the S T A R S acronym stand for?
· Who signed a blessing using the stars?
· Who was the first Hebrew to receive a Blessing Promise for all the families in the earth?
· What was the main blessing that came from Abraham's lineage?
· Why do you think that church attendance can help strengthen family relations?
· Do you believe there is evidence to prove church attendance is a major factor to strengthen family relations?
· What are two of your strengths?
· What are two of your weaknesses?
· What is your parenting big picture?
· What kind of life do you want to build for your children?
· Are your values helping bring your big picture to reality?
· Do your activities help to bring your big picture to reality?
· Will your lineage bring the same blessing, as did Abraham's?

Chapter 2

TOGETHER - BUILDING RELATIONSHIPS

"THE ABC'S OF BUILDING RELATIONSHIPS"
ATTACHING, BONDING, AND COMMUNICATING

CHAPTER 2

27

TOGETHER - BUILDING RELATIONSHIPS

"THE ABC'S OF BUILDING RELATIONSHIPS"
ATTACHING, BONDING, AND COMMUNICATING

Kite Talk :

Choosing the Fabric of love

Below are options for different styles of flying fabric for kites. Strong, yet compliant, fabric is good for flying in the wind; likewise, love and bonding are necessary elements for enduring relationships. After reading this section, choose a kite fabric and remove it from the kit.

Types of Fabrics:
- Thin fabric will not last for it is made for sunny days and thrills only.
- Thick fabric is too heavy, easily overcome by circumstances, too weighty and unable to stay in the air.
- Buoyant fabric has the ability to allow air to pass through and yet is tough enough to keep flying. The fabric of some kites is too thin to endure soaring for great lengths of time. What keeps our kites soaring is a question we want to answer during our child's early, formative years and then apply forever.
- Love fabric is touching, affectionate, interactive. Love is the most critical of all human needs and must be present when establishing bonding relationships.

Star Talk ☆

For enduring relationships, choose the fabric of love.

29

Love is the most critical ingredient of all for bonding connections. Love is the thing babies need most for healthy development.

In chapter 2, the Parenting Skills Manual lays out a plan to help you connect with your children. We call it the A B C's of Building Relationships; attachment, bonding and communication skills that connect a child to his world. Relationships are the interacting forces of life. Relationships begin when a child is born; he assimilates his world and responds. Relationships are the most important part of healthy development in young children. As the child grows, relationships take on innumerable faces and styles, known as communication styles and techniques. Studying communication styles helps an individual not only to communicate with others by using words but also to communicate with their heart as well. Relationships also become a picture-view whereby we may see our own self better and serve as an aid to strengthen our weaknesses and draw from our strengths.

A and B of Building Relationships (Attaching and Bonding)

We learn from others, and we see our blunders and hopefully move on to better ways of connecting. However, when someone does not attach, bond or learn proper communication, then relationships do not form as in the following story:

My name is Trader. I was found in a trash can. I wish they would have let me die. I was told that someone took me to a hospital, and eventually I was taken into an orphanage. (I guess the lady and man who came for me meant well.) I was nearly eight and had already experienced cocaine, alcohol, and life as the street bum goes. Well, it went good for a while at their home but soon I started climbing out of windows and now I am in jail for holding up a local convenience store. I really don't care to know who my parents are. It doesn't matter now.

In a similar case, I called the local prison asking about the welfare of a certain person. An officer informed me of his present condition, and I said to him, "Please be kind to him, he really doesn't belong in the prison. He just doesn't have anyone to help him with his personal affairs." To my astonishment, the officer replied, "Ma'am, 95% of these people in here do not have anyone. That is why most of them are here."

Choosing the Fabric Called Enduring Love
Love is what we all want!

Trader's scenario is a reality found in a police record. Making attachments and bonding in the first few years is critical for healthy development. Key findings include:

Building Healthy Relationships:
- Your relationship with your child is the foundation of his or her healthy development.
- Your child's development depends on both the traits he or she was born with and their experiences.
- All areas of development (social/emotional/intellectual/language/motor) depend on a child's interaction with others. What children experience, including how their parents respond to them, shapes their development as they adapt to their world. Love, above all other human needs, is the most critical to establish bonding connections.

Love is the thing babies need most for healthy development. A baby may never know how to respond to love, or another human being, without being loved. Attachment, bonding, and communication begin as soon as children are brought into the world. Research shows that a baby's ability to connect with another human being right away is critical as they began to assimilate light, touch, and sound. According to research, this bonding connection is the most critical of all for your child's healthy development. In these early months, without some form of human, ecstatic wooing by at least one person, the child may never unlock from their world and engage in another. These children are at high risk for becoming self-centered, aggressive individuals who can inflict injury without remorse.

Attending, gentle nudges early on in a child's life is like setting the child's thermostat which establishes their evaluation senses. Some studies show that ignored crying (crying which is allowed to continue until the child is angry) builds into the child the ability to become angry sooner and with greater intensity. In other words, parents who ignore their children's cries inadvertently help develop their child's temper. The little cries which are noticed soon and lovingly build a security in the child and makes parenting much more pleasant. When parents provide consistent routines, children are assured they will be taken care of, and consequently, the child's temperament will be milder and easier controlled.

To Mom and Dad, You have truly shown me what love is. "Its love on it's knees." We are certainly walking through some unknown paths. One thing is for sure, you have given us the greatest gift of all by showing us what it means to love your children, "Love on its knees." Thank you for loving Gregory and little Garrison.

With all our Love, Cherie' & Greg

A child's brain signals at which level of intensity their needs will be met. Very early in development, a child's brain then transforms the stimuli, or level of intensity, into personality traits. Temperaments, nurtured early, become compliant and loving if their needs are met with gentle nudges. There is no validity in the old saying, "Let a child cry or he will be spoiled."

- Right away you can notice what temperament (personality) your child is displaying by their crying patterns. Parental attendance to temperamental needs early on develops security, and continued nurturing early on helps build a behaved child and one who learns sooner.

Insights to Bring out the Shine – Consistency

Parents need to work on building a consistent lifestyle. Routines for meals, sleep, communication, physical exercise, and cleanliness help contribute to a consistent lifestyle. The following list of Age/Development Patterns shows the importance of regular routines to child development:

Age/Development Patterns

- 0-1 yr   Regular routines of eating and sleep patterns are beginning to develop.
- 1-2 yrs   Routines of time together learning fear, happiness, and other communicable emotions.
- 3-5 yrs   By this time, a child knows if he is in control or if you are. If he is in control, he knows he can throw tantrums and get his way. He knows you don't mean what you say. Trust factors are easily broken at this early age.
- 6-7 yrs   The basic human will has been formed.

Many basic child-rearing issues may be easily solved once parents understand the power of routine and consistency to a child's development.

Attaching Love's Heart Strings

The doctor placed the baby on Maria's stomach while he cut the umbilical cord. She watches him clip the attachment and wash the baby's eyes. "At last, there is no connection to my body," she thought to herself with a sigh of temporary relief. "I'm just me again, no strings attached."

But, somehow, just as she thought those words, she heard a little cry and sensed things would never be the same again. She looked at her son's soft red skin, she felt his faint heart beat, and then suddenly realized a tiny thread was hanging from his heart. Unmistakably, she checked again. Under the little onesie t-shirt and wrinkled skin, a dangling thread hung loose from her son's heart. "Oh, my," she winces. "We are still connected."

If this little invisible thread is not found and nurtured by an adult, it is possible the baby may not survive. Statistics prove that early attachments are the best nourishment for helping babies learn how to connect with other human beings. In fact, without proper connections made when the baby is just an infant, the baby may not survive.

You say to yourself, "Indeed, I will wrap this tiny heart string around mine. This baby is so helpless; its very life is depending on me." Gently, you connect the invisible thread as you kiss the baby over and over, and brush his cheek on yours. When you do this, a love story begins to intricately weave its fibers into every part of your heart.

Later, as the child grows into maturity, the relationship takes on the intricate art of letting go, which is also your child's only means of survival as a mature adult. Will your relationship endure and be strong? Only you and time can weave the story of this relationship like fabric that is being woven into a tapestry for all to see.

Attaching and Bonding

Attach the string to the heart of the kite.

Bonding is the most important attachment that ever can be made for healthy development. The three basic cords of love are God, parents, and children. When these three are intricately bonded together, they make possible the foundation for a strong family. A child with these three elements bonded together in His love fabric have the highest ratings for becoming a winner according to Heritage Foundation statistics (Fagan, 1998).

> A love story begins to intricately weave its fibers into every part of your heart.

Bonding is made up of routine attachments. For example, it is three o'clock in the morning and a little cry, sometimes softer than a whisper, awakens you. *"Oh yes,"* your mind registers, *"it is time for my baby girl's feeding."* You stretch and mentally wish you could go back to sleep, but she wins. One look at her dimpled smile and you know it's worth it. Maybe she is still just days old, just her mere need of sustenance wins. It is sometimes these not-so-pleasant feedings, baths, and consistent routines that create healthy attachments and bonding essential to healthy development.

For toddlers, routines and bonding are shining-star words because children learn through repetition. Children need order, space, and time for their thought processes to function. They have the ability to put patterns of time in order. Very early routines and patterns help them to be more cooperative and, in general, learn faster.

Holding On and Letting Go

Just as attachment and bonding are critical to a child's survival early on, the art of letting go becomes just as critical later. It's sort of a paradox… you hold on tightly only to find you have to let go. In comparison to the kite and string, the object is to hold the string taunt while allowing the kite to soar.

Star Talk ☆

Bonding the three basic cords of love - God, Parents and Children - the cement for a strong foundation.

Bonding and attachments are so closely intertwined that they cannot be separated. The art of parental holding on and later letting go is the child's only means of survival.

Attaching and Bonding Fabric

The importance of learning the cues in development is critical for healthy development. In flying a kite, if the fabric is too thin or too thick, endurance becomes limited.

Number one through five
for qualifying a bonding and attaching time.
With five being the highest.

Bonding & Attachment Builders	Bonding & Attachment Blockers
· Parents tend to child's needs	· Both parents work and drop baby off at sitter
· Routines	· Parents fail to build consistent patterns or routines
· Feedings	
· Show affection to each other and baby	· No affection or interchanging of affectionate wooing
· Talking, interacting	· Disconnection of emotion from child
· Attending church	
· Responsible parenting	· Parents do not go to church
· Bathing, dressing	
· Committed to values	· Quarreling
· Happy environment	· Harsh environment

Class Illustration

With a camera that has a roll of film, take many pictures at the beginning of the class. At the end of the class, take out the camera and unwind the film. The film that held so much potential and promise on its frames is destroyed. The point is, like those ruined pictures exposed inappropriately, improper care during the early stages of a child's development can ruin the possibilities for their entire life.

Kite Talk:

It is time to check out your kite kit again. Now that you have picked out the fabric of love for your kite, it is time to look at those two sticks in the kit. Actually, when you connect them to the kite as you see in the drawings, you will discover there are four different areas of the kite's fabric the sticks must be attached to in order for the kite to fly properly. Also, these four areas of the kite need to be balanced for it to fly. In parenting, we call this balancing of our lives the following four basic human needs: physical, mental, emotional, and spiritual. Have fun connecting your sticks to the fabric of love. It won't be long before we'll be ready for flight.

The "C" of Building Relationships (Communicating)

We have learned that the A's and B's of relationships are attaching and bonding. Now we are going to study the C which stands for communicating. The communication styles of a person are the potpourri splashes of their whole being. Who we are and how we express ourselves is a mix of our culture, temperament, values, fears, and accomplishments. When we shake it all up, it comes out in body language and in words. That is why "little" words are so big when it comes to communication.

May I relate to you a little story that sent a powerful message using a little kite.

The Electric Kite

During a thunderstorm in June of 1752, Benjamin Franklin sent a little kite into the air with a piece of wire attached to it. When lightening struck, he made a very amazing and powerful discovery… electricity travels.

Benjamin Franklin coined many words during his study of electricity, words such as battery, negative, positive, consensus, plus, and minus. In fact, we use many of these words today.

Words, like electricity, can be very powerful. They can be like a battery and hold charge or give charge. Words can be negative or positive, and they can be a consensus of the flow. Like Benjamin Franklin's electric kite, words carry a powerful charge.

Some of us have spent at least eighteen years of internship in parenting styles, and we become what we have been around; unless, through intervention and awareness, we make a conscious effort to do otherwise. Just as we evaluated our values to get the big picture for our life, we will now evaluate our communication styles. **How well we understand our** communication style will help us relate to ourself and to others.

Understanding Ourselves is the Key to Communication

Let's start with the four basic needs of humanity: physical, mental, spiritual, and emotional. Understanding ourselves in these four areas unlocks the doorway to understanding others. Notice that a kite has four different areas where balance is necessary for proper flying. As we examine each of these four areas in our lives, we discover both strengths and weaknesses. The key to making the chapters in this book work for you is asking, "Am I growing in these areas?" Growth is the key. Each area has needs that emerge at different times in our lives.

This concept is similar to Maslow's Hierarchy of Human Needs. Abraham Maslow proposed that human beings are motivated by unsatisfied needs, and that certain lower needs must be satisfied before higher needs can be satisfied. Maslow's theory basically says that physiological needs (basic needs such as hunger, thirst, etc.) must first be met. Then safety needs (shelter, clothing, protection, etc.) come second. Once safety needs are supplied, then and only then can love-esteem needs (relationships with family and friends) begin to be answered. Those three basic needs must be met in that order for self-actualization (who we are and our purpose in life) to be realized in an individual's life.

Our study, similar to Maslow's, looks at the four basic divisions which make up the human being: physical, spiritual, mental, emotional. While this information is not meant to be a thorough evaluation, it is meant to stimulate an awareness of human needs and consideration for growth.

Four Areas of Self-Examination

Analyze Related Terms	Strategize	Disciplining Factor	Personalize Goals
· **Physical**	Proper nutrition, rest, clothing, exercise, dental care, vision, hearing	Self Governing	Areas I need to improve (e.g. exercise 1 hour daily)
· **Mental**	Ability to think, rationalize, educate, rest, nurture understanding	Positive Thinking Self discipline Godliness	Take care of stress, Taking time for positive input (books, etc.), Evaluate mental growth.
· **Emotional**	Care, the seat of understanding temperament, social interaction, self-actualization, self worth .	Self Governing	Understanding myself to understand others, Evaluate stress, Find daily moments of rest
· **Spiritual**	Temperament, seat of self-actualization, values, standards of life, etc. Moral consciousness	Self-governing mind Godliness growth	Daily devotions, Prayer relationship, Personal relationship with God

Physical Health
Am I a responsible steward of my health?

- · Routine medical exams and taking care of dental, hearing , eyes, etc.
- · Taking care of ourselves physically is vital if we are taking care of others.
- · Routine exercises and eating healthy foods is for those who are concerned about endurance and making it to High Hopes Hill.
- · Improve physical appearance.

Mental Health

A healthy mental state is one of well being; rational soundness, a condition free from diseases of the mind. Mental and physical health are linked closely together. In fact, Webster's Dictionary defines health as mental and physical well being.

- Mental health is being able to make daily decisions without feeling overwhelmed, angry, and stressed.
- Do I have enough mental facilities to function in a safe fashion for myself and others?
- Do I read positive material to keep my mind challenged and active?
- Do I need to take classes to sharpen my mental awareness?
- Do I involve myself with positive experiences?

Emotional Health

How well we manage our emotions, especially in every day situations, is a sign of our maturity. The immature person is driven by emotion, while the mature person realizes that emotions change depending on the circumstance. In parents' lives, stress often drives emotions.

- Am I managing my stress well?
- What is stressing me?
- What do I spend my time doing?
- What happens when the kids get to me, and I am physically zapped? Do I breathe deep, count to 10, and call for a moment of isolation?

Spiritual Health

The condition of the spirit is essential to harmony of all other elements in our lives – physical, mental, and emotional. Spiritual health is the sense of the spirit being at peace. This brings to mind peace with whom and what? A person's spiritual make-up is intertwined with every aspect of a person's life. Thus, it is imperative that spiritual needs are met.

- What strong foundation am I standing on?
- Do I have a relationship in personal devotion?
- Am I at peace with God?
- Do I have a true relationship with Him through prayer and devotion?

- What value systems have my partner and I developed at home for caring for the children?
- What do I believe is the correct line of order for a home?
- How will we address issues when we conflict?
- What is acceptable behavior in terms of social interaction at home?
- What is acceptable behavior when we are speaking of words, actions, and facial expression?
- What kind of handles of address will I accept?
- What is good?
- What is evil?
- What spiritual guidelines have we made that will be the foundation for building our mutual agreements in child rearing?

I am talking; can anyone hear me?

In summary, getting our children to hear us is one thing, but transmitting understanding is another. We want our children to be winners. We want to set them up for the good life. However, if they are not hearing us or if they have selective hearing, how will we succeed in training them?

Getting our message across is all in the "C" word: Communication. Webster defines communication as: 1) interchanging thoughts or feelings, 2) to transmit as to transmit a disease: imparting thoughts, knowledge or information by writing or speaking, or art forms, body language.

Relationships are largely dependent upon effective communication. The whole unit of a family is built upon relating to one another. The better the relationship, the closer knit the family. Therefore, in parenting, the ability to draw from various communication skills will help one communicate messages more clearly and effectively.

Understanding that communication then is a conglomerate of visuals and sounds helps affirm the statement that children learn more from what they see you do than from what they hear you say.

"I can't hear you for your actions speak louder than your words."

40

The chart below describes the four temperaments along with their basic strengths and weaknesses. Our individual personalities or temperaments affect our communication styles.

The Four Temperaments - Personality Evaluations

	Strengths	Traits	Weaknesses
·Sanguine	Joyful and Outward	Giver	Impulsive and Messy
·Phlegmatic	Patient and Peaceful	Quiet	Low Motivation and Inward
·Melancholy	Talented and Affectionate	Moody	Inward
·Choleric	Leader Type, Organizer	Strong Willed	Commanding and Low Tolerance

Usually, most people are a mix of at least two or three temperaments with one being the strongest. If you are curious about knowing what your or your child's temperament is, you will find a personality test included in the appendix. Personality and temperamental differences between children and parents is an interesting study. It is also interesting to see what temperaments a husband and wife team has. Keep in mind the biblical view of temperaments found in Galatians 5:22-25 (that the spirit or temperament of man can be controlled by the infilling of God's Holy Spirit). Thus, the fruit of the Spirit – love, joy, peace, long-suffering, gentleness, goodness, faith, meekness, and self-control – become evident in that man's life and personality as he allows the Holy Spirit to temper the weakness of his human personality.

Spirit Controlled Temperament

Tim LaHaye wrote a book entitled *Spirit Controlled Temperament* that I recommend to parents for careful study. I also recommend *Personality Plus* by Florence Littauer for parents wishing to better understand temperaments and personalities. What is sad is a family where there are no spirit-controlled temperaments, and therefore, nothing to bridle the weaknesses. For example, I recall a household that had a very phlegmatic mother and choleric father. The phlegmatic mother continually hid the wrong doings of the children in order to have peace with the choleric father. The situation was disastrous. The children continued in their wrong doings and knew full well there would not be any consequences. When they became teenagers, they were the classic examples of those you hear of climbing out of windows, leaving home, and getting involved with drugs.

Kite Talk:

Spiral Downward – Caving-In Syndrome

The caving-in syndrome represents the moments of giving in. Some temperaments, such as impulsive sanguine or moody melancholy, have more of a giving-in nature. In a rage they may say to their child, "No TV for a month!" which is unrealistic. And then after much wearing down from the kids, they may give in and say, "Oh, who cares! Go ahead and watch what you want to. It's the only way I can get you to go to bed." Appeasing the whining or constant bickering shows others that the order of the home is lacking. Like the wolf in the story of the Three Little Pigs, who blew and blew until the house caved in. If the kids know you are going to give in they are going to blow and blow until you do. They know just how long you will hold out and how hard to blow. They are very skilled. It is much better to have pre-thought out disciplinary measures for offenses so you can effectively carry through with them. Otherwise, making calls set by moods is arbitrary discipline and confuses the children.

Star Talk ☆

A Godly spirit-controlled temperament is like a thermostat. When our temperament needs to be adjusted, a life of spirit-controlled temperament allows the Holy Spirit to adjust the natural human spirit, then the adjusting turns for the good.

Personality Grid

Personality	Strengths & Emotions	Weaknesses	At Work
Sanguine	Joyful, makes home fun, people lover	Impulsive, brassy, forgetful, interrupts, angered easily, messy	Creative, energetic, catalyst for new jobs, storyteller, good host at parties
Phlegmatic	Calm, avoids conflicts, good under pressure, diplomat	Low-motivation, blank, mumbles, compromising	Patient, persistent, does a good job working in routines
Choleric	Determined, exerts leadership, knows the right answer	Domineering, argumentative, tactless	Goal oriented, delegates, good salesman or leader,
Melancholy	Compassionate, self-sacrificing, deep feeler	Analytical, resentful, withdrawn, too sensitive, manipulator	Perfectionist, sees the problems, good musician, writer, etc.

Most people are usually a mix of at least two or more personalities with predominance in one. What makes an interesting study is two people getting married and blending their dominating characteristics together within the home. This is where the Biblical account of the Holy Spirit comes into great need. If both the husband and wife are dedicated to allowing God's Spirit to temper the weaknesses within their personalities and help them to be more Christ-like, then their home will have harmony. The following Grid for Parenting Blends explains some of the different combinations of parental personality blends, the problems that can arise from those dynamics, and how to resolve them.

A Grid for Parenting Blends

		Combinations of Personality's	Spirit Controlled
Sanguine Mom	Choleric Dad	Mom's joyfulness may irritate dad's goals and loud arguments may result in front of children.	Dad needs to talk to mom and ask her to help him reach goals with children and she needs to assess her responsibilities and comply
Phlegmatic Mom	Choleric Dad	Mom's laid back nature and dad's lack of tact can cause phlegmatic mom to hide children's mistakes. This leads to disobedient children.	Mom needs to realize she is going to hinder children trusting them as parents. She needs to quit hiding and confront dad alone, if need be, and continue to discipline
Choleric Mom	Phlegmatic Dad	Mom's goal-oriented nature can be mistaken for bossiness by dad and a resentful environment results because dad does not participate in disciplining.	Dad needs to become more alert, assess his duty and fulfill his role as dad. Mom needs to assess and rely upon dad.
Melancholy Mom	Sanguine Dad	Dad's fun, impulsive personality was fun in courtship, but now he grows angry quickly and melancholy mom can become depressed unless some help is given to direct dad to fulfill his responsibilities.	Mom needs to emphasize the need for dad to assess his responsibilities and assume his role. While he is fun, he needs to balance and assess his responsibility

Try the Personality Temperament Test for Fun

Place the number 1, 2, 3, 4, or 5 by each personality characteristic, with 5 being the strongest and 1 the weakest. Score and look at the personality grill to find your strongest temperament

·Sanguine	Socialize	Charmer	Impulsive
·Phlegmatic	Monotonous Jobs	Systematic	Very Laid Back
·Choleric	Good Salesman	Strong willed	Can be domineering
·Melancholy	Servant Spirit	Compassionate	Whiner

Notes

_____

_____

_____

_____

_____

_____

_____

"The Power of a Little Word, a Little Boy and a Kite"

The Homan Walsh Kite Story - Used with permission from www.thekitestore.com

Because of one little boy who flew a kite over a gorge, the Niagara Bridge was erected across Niagara Falls in 1847.   A Philadelphia architect, Charles Ellett, received the contract to design and build the bridge across Niagara Falls. He accepted and his first challenge was that of connecting a 700 ft. wide gorge. He first thought that a single rope could pull the first cable across and that a string might be able to carry the first rope over. This brought to his mind the idea of using a kite. He decided to have a kite flying competition. It was during this competition that Homan Walsh flew his kite connecting the American gorge to the Canadian. Because of one little boy who thought he could, the mighty gulf was spanned. His obstacles were obvious: high winds, craggy rocks, and great depths of boiling, whirling rapids with waters exceeding 40 miles per hour in their sweep. Yet, because he took the challenge, today we have the ability to cross this gorge on a beautifully constructed bridge.

Dealing with relationships is like flying a kite. We have obstacles such as many individuals whose viewpoints come from opposite ends of the spectrum. However, with a string of faith and a few flying tips, it is possible to bridge relationships by crossing over the gapping holes and craggy rocks. Instead of falling into the same pitfalls that leave scars, wounds, and generational crevices, wouldn't you rather build a bridge for the generations who follow after you to overcome rivers of broken places?

The Four Kites of Communication Styles

Heidi the High Flyer Kite
- Consistent
- Active listener
- Upward upwords
- Builds affirmation
- Uses reflective words - never attacks child, but uses "I feel"...
  "When you do not pick up your toys, it makes me feel very sad."
- Flies on love and open ended acceptance.

Heidi the High Flyer

Nan the Nodder Kite
- · Passive listener
- · Always standing there nodding, never showing interest
- · Always continues in what they are doing
- · Nodding or nagging

Nan the Nodder

Henry the Hurler Kite
- · Impulsive distant
- · Downwards and downwords
- · Conversations offer no response, just phrases
- · Spiraling downward; sink into slough of despondency

Henry the Hurler

Sam the Sock Kite
- · The sock-it to them communication
- · Slaps, hits, yells

Passive Listener vs. Aware Listener - An Analogy

Nan, the nodding kite, just hangs in the air, nodding in the wind and never going anywhere in the sky. She just nods and does not produce active listening or participate with any real interaction.

Close relationships thrive when one believes another is truly listening with their heart as well as their eyes and ears. The next two examples illustrate the difference between passive listeners and aware listeners. Henry the Hurler is an inattentive and self-absorbed parent whose passive listening style communicates complete indifference to his child. Heidi the High-flyer, on the other hand, represents the parent who is an active listener, attentive and interested, whose active style communicates real concern for her child.

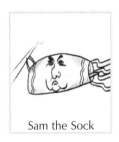

Sam the Sock

A. Passive Listener

Illustrated in this small skit is a man sitting in a chair reading a newspaper when his child comes bouncing in from school. (Passive listening is exemplified when the man does not put down the paper as the child is showing her daddy the work she did at school.) Daddy continues to read paper and nods head approvingly at the child at the same time. After several attempts to get dad's attention, daddy disapprovingly says, "I told you yes, now go on outside and play while I read my paper." The child shows her sadness by puckered lips and flowing tears.

B. Aware Listener

Heidi the high flyer kite. Mother is sitting in a chair, reading the newspaper, when her child comes bouncing in from school. "Look, Mommy, at what I did at school." Mommy Heidi promptly puts down the paper and exclaims happily, "Oh, Mark, that paper shows a lot of hard work. Wow!" Heidi rubs Marks head and kisses him on the cheek, takes paper and places it on the refrigerator. Mark shows his happiness at receiving the affirmation by smiling and jumping in glee.

Star Talk ☆

Research finds communication that is aware and active builds self-esteem and a sense of security in children and is thought to be one of the keys to helping children learn faster and make friends easier.

An aware listener is one who hears with his eyes, heart, and head.

Reflective Communication

This type of communication uses feeling words instead of attacking words. It shows empathy. It shows your child that you are trying to understand what they feel like inside. While you do not base your decisions on feeling principles, your style of communication should show feeling words. Words such as sad, happy, bubbly, joyful, are feeling words.

Sam the Sock

Sam the Sock Kite... always socks it to them.
"You spilled your milk." "You are bad." "You did not clean your room." "You did not do your homework." "You are a lousy kid."

Heidi the High Flyer

Heidi the High Flyer Kite

Comments to them on how it makes her feel first and then tells them what behavior she needs. Example: "I need you to clean your room. When it is messy, it makes me feel very sad."

Levels of Communication ~ How close or trusted is your style?

Expressive and open-ended conversation builds trust and communication level. Reporting and closed-ended communication builds barriers and shrinks communication level.

Rob the Robot Kite

This robot models deadpan expressions. He never gets involved; consequently, his children will model the same expressions. He stays on the level of reporting such as "Don't touch," "The weather is nice," "Stop it," "Yes," "No," etc.

Rob the Robot

Heidi the High Flyer Kite

She decorates room with expression. She squeals with delight and happiness as she touches each decoration. "How beautiful." "Grandma gave me that one." Consequently, Heidi will pass on upward words and expressions of love.

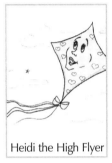

Heidi the High Flyer

Herman the Hanger Kite

He always gets hung up on issues and never comes down from his tree until everyone is worn out. He does all the talking and never lets anyone else have a chance. He never listens. His kite is stuck and all he does is keep his accelerator in motion.

Parenting Communication and Star Affirmation Words

Solving conflicts using a star method.

Weekly family meetings help foster communication skills. If your family lives a hectic lifestyle, schedule a time at least once a week for the entire family to be together, like Monday nights or Sunday afternoons, so everyone can get together. Communication is best in person and strong relationships thrive on communication. These times of communication and affirmation will go a long way toward solving family conflicts and issues when they occur.

Herman the Hanger

When conflict arises within the family, keep in mind critical issues need to be handled privately, especially when the conflict is with one family member. Seek to isolate that person; never to embarrass him in front of family members. In a private manner, give words of affirmation first, then listen to the problem attentively and openly. After you have listened, then you may say, "I understand…" and repeat your understanding of the conflict. After you are sure you have heard it correctly, tell them you will need time to consider the solution or you will need to get with husband or wife.

Always seek and speak to affirm relationships.

Below are steps for solving conflicts if more than one member of the family needs to be involved. This type of decision making may begin with questions like, "Where will the next vacation be?" or "What will be the next family night recreation?"

Five Step Star methods to solve conflict

1.   **S**peak affirming words such as, "I understand where you are coming from, but have you considered…" (Then say what your idea is). Leave out down words and curse words, which harm communication and damage relationships.

2.   **T**ogether agree to show respect by waiting until one person is finished talking before speaking.   Interrupting shows disrespect. Always speak privately if there is only one person involved.

3   **A**ttentively listen to the problem and repeat the problem to the person speaking to make sure you heard them correctly.

4   **R**aise possible solutions from the individual person or everyone in the family.

5   **S**how consideration for everyone's ideas by saying you think they are all very thought-provoking ideas, and you and your spouse will consider all the options and talk to everyone soon.

Always stand on your values of home relationships by insisting that everyone show kindness to each other. Reaffirm with words of understanding.

Kite Kit Toolbox:

Vocabulary Toolbox for Chapter 2

"Don't get hung up on hang-ups"

Phrases and Words are important in studying Communication Skills for Relationships
·   Overcoming obstacles in relationships
·   Communication Obstacles

- ·   Idiosyncrasy
- ·   Personality
- ·   Personality Clash
- ·   Personality Types

Terms to be familiar with:
Webster defines …
Idiosyncrasy - Personal habits peculiar to or distinctive of a particular individual
Semantics: Arising from different meanings or interpretation of words
Cultural - Having to do with one's behavior or beliefs characteristic of a particular social, ethnic, or age group
Personality - The sum total of the physical, emotional, mental, and social characteristics of an individual
Personality clash - When people have different ideas of handling something, but both think they are right because of a natural tendency to handle it from their basic personality temperament.
Personality Types: - Referring to the basic four personality types - Sanguine, Choleric, Phlegmatic, and Melancholy

Overcoming power struggles: Conflicts. When there is a problem, keep the focus on the problem and not on each other. This is like flying the Diamond kite.
Idiosyncrasies are as different as people. Idiosyncrasies are mannerisms. They are quirky habits, such as a loud voice, assertive personality, going out of the way to do a particular thing, like holding your head in a certain way when you laugh or smile. Realizing that everyone has mannerisms or ways about them that make them unique will help us not to take things so personally and be easily offended. For example, when Ted is asked to make a decision, he stares at the ceiling before making up his mind. Someone who does not know Ted may think Ted is being rude. However, to anyone who knows Ted, that is just Ted's way.
Semantics is the way language and expressions change over time or with regard to region such as expressions that are relevant to a particular area. Take for example, the expression, "Cut the onions." To a southerner, when you tell the restaurant assistant to cut the onions, you are saying, "Would you please leave out the onions?" In the north, when you say cut the onions, they literally think you mean to cut the onions, as in cut them or chop them up.

Star Talk ☆

Kites catch the updraft and fly; however, kites that catch the downward draft spiral out of control and fall to the earth.

Power Words for Catching the Updraft
Webster defines:

- Trust: The basis for building a relationship
- Love: Feeling of warm personal attachment or deep affection necessary for the foundation of a relationship
- Fair: To handle with justice
- Honor: Fairness or integrity in one's beliefs and actions
- Forgive: To grant pardon or remission of an offense
- Respect: Admiration, proper acceptance or courtesy
- Relationship: A significant association between people or things
- Unity: U - n – I the state of being one. Oneness.

Kite Talk:

Evaluation for Chapter 2 - Let's Fly

What are the A B C 's relationship building blocks?

_____

What are the 4 basic communication styles discussed in this chapter?
1. Heidi

_____

2. Nan

_____

3. Sam

_____

4. Henry

_____

Fill in the Name

Aware	Listens with Heart	Reflective Thinking	Open Words

_____

Passive	Just nods without looking up from what he is doing	Disinterested	Closed Words

_____

Give these a Name:

·   Hung up on hang ups: _____

·   Likes to sock it to them: _____

·   Which is the balanced Parenting Communication style?

_____

·   Why?

_____

Reflective Thinking and Feeling Words

Rather... "When you don't do your work it makes me feel"...
_____ how?

Listening is a vital part of communication _____yes
_____no

Respectful
communication
makes
respectful
relationships.

10 Up-words for flying kites and kids upwards
1.   I love you!
2.   Great job!
3.   Honey, how about a hug?
4.   Always do your best!
5.   That's good, but let's try that again.
6.   Awesome work!
7.   You belong to me, and I belong to you.
8.   Let's go together.
9.   Way to go!
10.   You are shining tonight!

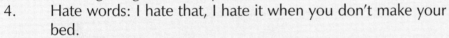

10 Down-words that bring kites and kids downwards

1. Dummy.
2. You will never be anything.
3. You're getting more like your dumb old uncle.
4. Hate words: I hate that, I hate it when you don't make your bed.
5. If you don't stop, I'm going to slap you.
6. Negative name calling is mental abuse and injures sometimes for life.
7. Freckle face.
8. Shut-up!
9. Get one of the bigger kids, not you, you shrimp.
10. You'll never amount to anything.

Chapter 3

ABILITIES
"USING THE SHINE PLAN"
LEADERSHIP, TALENTS, ACADEMICS, AND TIME

C
H
A
P
T
E
R

3

57

ABILITIES
"USING THE SHINE PLAN"
LEADERSHIP, TALENTS, ACADEMICS, AND TIME

Star Talk ☆

Developing mental ability or talent and not developing character is like placing an atomic bomb on the top of a child's head and applauding his grand ability to carry it across the room. What a foolish parent to try this trick. Yet, everyday we see this enacted.

The Shine Plan of Action

We are all aware of parents scurrying to saddle their kids up to the latest new thing whether it is T-ball, gymnastics, soccer, sports, or literary competitions. We know if high achievement was the equation to success in America's homes, there wouldn't be the rapid decline that is evident in today's culture. Please do not misunderstand this unit on the "Shine Plan." While I am trying to encourage parents to find their children's talents, and help develop them, I equally believe biblical character and spiritual growth must be taught. The "Shine Plan" is actually a plan to provide balance while proceeding over the pitfalls of puberty.

So where do you start as parents to build character in your child? How do you put the "want to" inside that little lump of clay? I absolutely agree that no one is perfect. We humans are always left searching for answers. However, the quest is the part of the journey that parents must endure in order to gain victory. While you cannot force love or learning, you can seek the keys to nurture the shine.

Keeping power struggles away and building confidence between you and your child creates a loving atmosphere where the best happens. I really believe every child has unique talents and skills. If we find his learning style, his temperament, and something he likes to do then we can help him soar over the pitfalls of adolescence to become a winner with a bright future.

In this chapter, I want to talk from my heart about a variety of characteristics and how, as parents, we can look for ways to diagnose children's needs and then create a positive plan of action.

In general, when we speak of a child's need to grow, we are speaking of growing spiritually, academically, developing their talents, and combining this with leadership characteristics.

We must first "think" what we would like our children to become and never say it is impossible. Rather, think of one thing they may begin right away to learn. The journey of a thousand miles begins with the first step.

59

The strength and quality of your relationship with your child has more power than any discipline technique.
— Cynthia Tobias

Time magazine published a cover story in February, 2005 entitled, "Pushy Dads, Hovering Moms, Parents Who Don't Show Up at All -- Are Kids Paying the Price?" (February 21, 2005). The authors of the article brought up issues of major concern to teachers of America's children. For example, teachers say they no longer can correct or tell students what they need to study because of a mom or dad who will defend the student.

After being a director of a Christian school for over 25 years, serving with educational offices of the state, and having worked on Governor Ruth Ann Minner's Work Task for Early Childhood, I have a growing concern over this trend of a lack of willingness from parents to take the responsibility of overseeing their children. In the end, the children will be the losers. For instance, in the graph in the first chapter of this book, we saw the constant decline in homes rise when jobs and education take priority over the home. Another problem is the growing status quo of broken homes where live-ins and or second and sometimes third marriages try to create some semblance of family unity. Discipline is often lacking in these situations because no one wants the children to experience consequences from the other guardians. Many parents do not want their children to experience any kind of consequences and resist other authority figures in their children's lives. This same spirit has carried over into the schools and churches of our nation. More and more parents are threatening instead of using teamwork.

Many parents struggle working to pay for what they are giving their children when what their children really need - time with them - cannot be bought. I have even heard parents say, "I don't want to be there when the kids come home." By the time parents do get home, most of the time this kind of home has already begun to unravel. The article written in the above-referenced TIME magazine speaks loud and clear about what is going on in American homes and family relationships today.

How do you turn on that motor inside your children for the good and set them up to become winners? You start by putting together their needs for spiritual growth, hidden talent, academic achievement, and leadership development. This basic philosophy, which is not new to educators, takes on a different flavor at home.

Yesterday's Carrot, Donkey, and Stick Philosophy is No Longer Being Used

In years past, the carrot, donkey, and stick philosophy was used in education. The carrot (incentive) was held in front of a donkey and a stick (consequence) swatted him from behind. Together, these double motivations kept the donkey focused on forward motion. Sadly, in today's society, it seems the carrot is now something of high monetary value and the stick is all but disappearing. For the carrot to motivate the donkey, the donkey had to be hungry. When the donkey's appetite waned, a swat of the stick kept him moving. With no stick (consequence), the donkey will move sporadically at best or fall off a cliff at worst -- a frustrating prospect to say the least. Incentives without consequences equal sporadic motivation.

You Can Unwrap the Shine ... It Starts At Home

I believe the secret to keeping the child moving forward and unwrapping the shine is found inside the child. As parents take the responsibility and diligently seek to uncover what motivates their child, they will hold in their hands a golden key to the doors of their child's life. You cannot hand the keys of a car over to your two year old and say, "Here, honey, have at it." The power is not age appropriate. However, there is power behind each stage/age which a child longs to hold. The secret is to find the appropriate turn-on. By two years of age, children are already developing definite patterns of favorite toys. You can even notice how some songs, pictures, books, or movies will hold their attention while others will not. These are definite patterns that you want to follow for their unique motivation turn on. The rest of this chapter is dedicated to help you unwrap the "Shine" doors of your child: his hidden talents, his favorite interests, and best academic learning styles in your child. Also, included is building the Bee-liever's family of character.

The technique of using an innate need to serve as a motivator is used as soon as a child is born by giving them their bottle. The bottle is a need, but also serves as a motivator to help them sleep. Different stimulants help to settle a child down and keep them headed in the right direction. As they get older, instead of always offering a new gimmick or money, the twist of the "Shine" plan is fueled by incentives innately built within; hidden talent, character, and positive learning outcomes.

5 Secrets of Unwrapping the "Shine"

S Start the process of building your child's Shine Profile (the unique styles of learning and interest unique to your child) 1-3 years... processing years.

H Hidden talent unique to child (defined) start to develop.

I Interest, academics, responsibilities, recreation.

N Natural new life doors. (next age appropriate freedom-responsibility)

E Everyone enjoy the "Shine". "Celebrate your child's achievements in a positive direction."

The Shine Plan

Using the next door of life for motivations (talent and age-appropriate responsibilities) become the incentive and leverage for keeping the child moving forward. The information needed to develop your child's "Shine Plan" must gathered which includes interests unique to your child. (Please look ahead the chart marked Child's Shine Profile.) After you have created your Child Shine Profile, you then incorporate your child's "Shine Action Plan" which will use to guide, motivate, and discipline them through the doors of life.

Remember, in keeping with our kite theme, the string of the kite must be h firmly while giving some release for freedom. This is the tricky part. The Sh Plan, when used daily and broken down into time segments, offers a han on the task of teaching character and academics. It will also help develop child's hidden talent.

Below is a step-by-step example for gathering information to create a "Sh Action" plan for yourself and your child.

Building a Child's Shine Action Plan Profile
Include which discipline technique works best overall for your child.

_____

Incorporate "The Next Door" incentive plan.

_____

(Shine Plan incorporates gathered information from above and uses it to put together your child's personal Shine Plan... the place he excels best.)

Life's Doors of Discipline

S	H	I	N
Shine Profile What is his age? What is his basic temperament? What does he like to do in his creative moments? What is his best learning style? Which disciplining consequental plan works best for him?	**Hidden Talent** To Be Developed Incentive (recreation) Character Responsibility Self-discipline Self-control Practice time Discipline/ Consequence	**Incorporate Academics** Incentive Recreation Character taught Responsibility Self-discipline Self-control Disciplining Consequences before progressing	**New Life Doors** Freedoms/ Responsibilities Age/Stage appropriate **E** **Enjoy the Shine** Celebrate

Moving Through the Doors of Life With "Shine in Mind"

In life, when we face something new, we may say, "We have found a new door." In the "Shine Plan," we say we have found the "Shine." In the next few pages, it is my desire to take you on an upward journey discovering talents and expanding horizons of possibilities for your child. As we build your child's profile - the way he learns best, his talents, and his hobbies - we open the doorways to new rooms for his life. The doors offer double motivation through a life incentive and a disciplining consequence. Other techniques of discipline are adaptable to this program. Parents can keep their child moving through the doors of life with his "Shine in Mind."

Shine Plan

Every home must have a functioning level; one where each person plays his role. As the leader, the parent keeps the wheels of progress turning in the child's life by using two basic aspects of motivational incentives. First is his interest in talent and second is his recreational life. These aspects are different for each child. In order for the parent to be successful in helping the child meet their responsibilities, the parent must know these key motivational elements in their child.

Developing Character through the
Motivational Doors of Talent and Recreation

These two words become the motivational doorway which open up leadership and learning skills for your child. They also serve as a restraining leverage for you to keep him moving on to the next door of life.
(This technique is explained in more detail later in this chapter.)

Moving through the Doors of Life with the **"Shine in Mind"** - Example
- **S -** Johnny's interest in talent and in recreation. (child's shine profile) motivation (1st door)
- (Progress through 1st door) Reaching for age level 9 while still only age 8
- **H -** At 8 years of age, parent says, "Johnny, which instrument would you like to try?"
- Make an appointment to go check out an instrument, starting with renting to buy. The goal of owning his very own instrument should be used as leverage to inspire practice and effort.
- **I -** Teach him the responsibilities of self-discipline, practice schedules and self-control (2nd door)

Keeping power struggles away and building confidence between you and your child creates a loving atmosphere where the best happens.

63

Keeping power struggles away and building confidence between you and your child creates a loving atmosphere where the best happens.
Cynthia Tobias

- Interest style for academic learning, responsibility, and character may be worked in the middle, before your child enjoys (next door) his high interest recreation.
- **N -** New responsibility or interest (Last door). This could be enjoying a friend coming over on Friday. According to age/stage, it may be looking forward to gaining the freedom and responsibility to drive the family car.
- **E -** Enjoy the "Shine" by celebrating in a positive way. (Take Johnny to a nursing home to play his instrument.)

 My Child's Shine Profile

Name: _____

Age: _____

Basic Personality Type: _____

Best Learning Style: _____

What you want them to excel in?

Academically: _____

Character: _____

Talent: _____

In sports he/she likes: _____

In music he/she would like to play: _____

He/She likes to hum and sing with the music: _____

He/She likes to speak: _____

He/She loves poetry and likes to read: _____

He/She enjoys crafts: _____

Train and move forward by Door of Life Incentive Shine Plan blending natural (personal style) life incentives with consequences.

Leadership Character

Join the Bee Family and become all you can bee.

Maintaining a Bee-lieving Environment:

What will my children remember about me as their parent?

The other day in the Circle Christian School Weekly Newsletter, I read an article by John Woodall entitled, "Dad's First Day in Heaven."

My mind went into great wonder. What happened right after his last breath? Did angels come and usher him right into the presence of God? Did he hear? What did he see? A serious question was asked by Tim Elmore to challenge this church. What would they remember, or would they remember you as always being the one to be right? Were we always trying to prove a point?

Parenting is serious; yet it is important for us to remember that, yes, we will blow it at times, and we are not always right. The important thing is for the kids to remember we are trying, above all, to have a close relationship with them, loving them beyond anything they do or say, even if we don't agree with their deeds.

Building Star Character "Shine"

II Peter 1:5-8, "And beside this, giving all diligence, add to your faith, virtue; and to virtue knowledge; and to knowledge, temperance; and to temperance, patience; and to patience, godliness; and to godliness, brotherly kindness; and to brotherly kindness, charity. For if these things be in you, and abound, they make you that ye shall neither be barren or unfruitful in the knowledge of our Lord Jesus Christ."

In your home, practice keeping all of the attributes listed in the verse above. Build your house upon faith and add all the attributes as pillars (virtue, knowledge, self-control, patience, godliness, brotherly kindness, and love). If, as parents, you endeavor to model these values in your home and insist your children live by them as well, you will have a strong home with a healthy environment free for bee-lieving and character growth.

Be a Bee-Liever...
The best environment is one that believes and is trusting.
First of all, this unit is designed for everyone. Perhaps you may think it's too late or impossible for your children to develop character.
Let me ask you to undo your thinking.

Think Outside the Box

How many boxes do you see?"
Please do not say 20. Look again, and notice the question,
"How many boxes do you see?"
One answer is 30, but another is 100.

If you look at a situation and think you will be succumbed by that situation, think again.

There are 100 reasons not to think there are only 20 squares above. There are many possibilities that can be achieved if we look beyond the obvious.

In chapter one, we dealt with parental baggage. Perhaps this is your third marriage, and you have children from each. Perhaps this is your first marriage and your child is only two years old. Whatever the case, remove all negative thoughts and go with me on a trip to the Bumble Bee Factory.

What is the Bumble Bee Factory?

The bumblebee factory is the factory where bees are made.
The master designer wanted everyone to know that he was making
something that even the highest performing rocket scientist would
have to agree… should not happen.
That is, He wanted the Bumblebees to fly…

But the Bumblebee cannot fly!

All the little flies and other flying creatures
would not believe this bee could fly….
For this bee was too big to fly!
This bee was not shaped to fly!
The Bumblebee could not fly…

But guess what?
The bumblebee can fly!

The Master Designer made the bumblebee's ears so he could
not hear all the negative remarks…

And this Bumblebee told all of his friends that he could fly,
and guess what his friends said to themselves,
"If he can fly, then we can fly"…

And they told all their friends
and friends,
you know the rest.

Now all the bumblebees in the bee family can fly.

Glenda Andrus

Official Kite Flyer Certificate

"Shine"

Member of the Bee Family

"I am better than a bumblebee"
I Bee-Lieve I CAN FLY!
This certificate, hereby certifies that,

(Parent's Name) _____

agrees to the following:

_____

I _____ , agree that as of today

_____ (date), the parents of, _____ ,

_____ and _____

agree to do as much as the bumblebee and overcome anything that
will keep me out of the air.
I agree to find at least one thing my child does well and promote his practice time

_____ , and day by day he will grow self-esteem.

He will grow character for I agree to train him in a particular life lesson such as

one hour on _____ each week.

His/Her self-esteem will flourish!

Signed _____
(kite flyer)

I am better than the bee!
This bee certificate is good for growing flyers, any shape, size, or color.
My child will grow in these areas - character, talent, and academics.
My pledge as a Bee Parent is to Bee there, to bee a model Bee, and Bee-lieve in my child.
I promise to bee a provider helping him/her to bee productive!

Maintaining a Bee-lieving Attitude

The Star Method, related below, helps parents fill their child's environment with happy memories and helps their children possess those productive leader-type characteristics.

Instilling Values "Star Leadership Character"

Stand : (Model what you preach)

The word, stand, in chapter one is the firm ground of values and a life of purpose on which the foundation of your home is built. The best principle you can follow is to live what you hand out. In other words, walk the talk and model what you want your children to become.

Together:

Teach children character traits that will help them to become people friendly (not people pleasers) and to have lasting relationships. This involves teaching them the art of standing their ground on convictions, but, at the same time, not becoming argumentative and always trying to prove a point. Benjamin Franklin was considered to be the great communicator for he skillfully negotiated. He was influential in settling great debates between countries. Perhaps we could learn from this art…

Sally said, "The meeting was a complete disaster. I do not think there is any use in having such a meeting." Sam answers, "I know what you mean, Sally. There was a lot of confusion, but have you ever thought of it this way, unless we have a meeting and bring out different views, we may never know how to help one another."

Teach your children appropriate conversation subjects. Any topic that can have strong biases is not good food for conversations with their friends.

Ability:

Help your children achieve to their fullest academically and help them find, develop, and enjoy their talents as an added enrichment to life. Build character using the fruits of the Spirit (love, joy, peace, long suffering, gentleness, temperance, goodness, meekness; Galatians 5:22) as your teaching points.

Responsibility:

Identify and teach your children the art of responsibility. Taking ownership for one's actions is vital for a life of purpose. Enjoying freedom or suffering consequences comes from the choices we make about responsibility.

Some attitudes are caught more than taught.

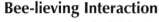

Bee-lieving Interaction
(For Parents and Children: Activity for Growth and Interaction)
  Choose a Biblical, Christian or government leader who showed virtue. Do a biography together of their life. Some suggestions are Jonathan Edwards, George Washington, Abraham Lincoln, or your pastor.

- Define honesty, truth, initiative
- What are the results of truth… trust?
- How can these traits be applied to a young person?
- What will happen when someone trusts you?
- Will you gain more freedom?
- With freedom, will you be required to bear more responsibility?
- You can talk about the day approaching in their lives when they will earn more responsibility – explain what's next.
- A 12-year-old may get to go on an overnight stay with a friend.

Responsibility in conversation and in deed.
This leads to the next freedom
- 15-year-old being able to obtain driver's permit.
  Responsibility – Freedom
  16-year-old driver's license – Responsibility
  Freedom and so on.
- When responsibility is neglected, what happens to trust and freedom?
- Courage: Does your child have the courage to do what is right among his peers?
- Can they do what is right without preaching to their friends?
- Courage is the opposite of being afraid.
- Talk about someone who was afraid to stand for ethical principles or Biblical principles and what happened to them.
- Teach them it is okay to be different, even if a popular person does the wrong thing.
- Think of Biblical examples such as Daniel or Esther.

Still Bee-lieving - The Family of Bee's
- **Bee Faithful:** Keep faith in your home environment. For by faith do we believe the worlds are framed. Faith gives you power to envision beyond normal circumstances to the possibilities.

- **Bee Prayerful:** A praying home usually stays together and over-comes obstacles. Prayer is the most powerful weapon for parents to use for their home and children.
- **Bee Virtuous:** Conform one's life to ethical principles, moral excellence, power, honesty, truth, and initiative.
- What moral principal did George Washington have that set him apart? Honesty.
- After marriage, our sons and daughters will have the job of tak-ing care of their own affairs. While they are in our household, clearly it is our responsibility to train them to become responsi-ble leaders. Your child will either be a follower or a leader. Wouldn't it be best if they could lead others?

Interaction for Age Appropriate Teen or Pre-teen *(around 12)*
Tim Elmore's website www.growingleaders.com gives these suggestion:
- Take a walk through a cemetery and observe the headstones.
- Ask questions about the number of years and read the epitaphs
- When you finish your walk, sit down and talk about what you observed.
- Ask questions like: What do you think life is all about? What would you like to do with your life that you would like others to remember?
- Then say, "Do you see why honesty, truth, love, etc. are very important?" Talk about it some more.

Bee-Knowledgeable
  "Study to show thy self approved unto God, a workman that needeth not to be ashamed, rightly dividing the word of truth…" (2 Timothy 2:15). This is a good time to make sure you have selected a talent that your child is working on. Academic training is usually routine but it takes more than the academics to build character. You can educate a young man but he can become a thief unless his life is molded by moral truths and under-girded by consistent consequences for wrongdoing.

Enhance His Spiritual Growth with Basic Training in the Word of God
- Can your children list the books of the Bible?
- Do they know basic Bible history?
- Can they cross reference Bible verses?

Enhance Practical, Everyday Skills

- Do they make their beds? (This is training for the 5-year old and should be expected by the time they are 7.) Set the bar high, and you will get high results; set the bar low, and you will get none.
- Older children should be expected to dust, clean, vacuum, mow the lawn, take out the trash, help with kitchen duties, etc.
- Gardening, sewing, cooking, painting, etc.
- Tool box basics – screw driver, wrench, measuring tape, etc.
- Money management
- Take each of the characteristics above and think of ways you can explore and teach them consistently to your children.

I highly recommend Pam Forster's (1995) book for sons, *Plants Grown Up*. It has enough material in it to keep a houseful of children busy from the day they can recite a memory verse until the day they get married. While this book is written mostly for boys, girls can benefit too. I also recommend the book she has written for girls entitled, *Polished Cornerstones*.

Notes

Kite Kit Toolbox:

Bee Words

- Bee Temperate
- Bee Patient
- Bee Godly
- Bee Forgiving
- Bee Kind
- Bee Loving

Bee Temperate: Self-restraint, self-control. Activity: Practice self-control by not interrupting each other at the dinner table. Write a paragraph of what self-control means to you and give an example of someone who shows self-control. How about appetite? Purity? Finances?

Bee Patient: Waiting without complaining or loss of temper - a form of being faithful. Why do we say, "The patience of Job?" For an activity, plant a seed in a cup. Water it and place it by a window. When it finally grows, we will see what it means to have patience.

Bee Godly: Teaching your children to have the characteristics of Godliness is teaching the attributes of being Godly and modeling obedience and reverence for God.
-        Honoring His Word
-        Studying His Word
-        Honoring the Sabbath day and keeping it holy
-        Recognizing and repenting of sin

Bee Forgiving: Forgiveness is the maintenance tool for every relationship to last.

Bee Kind: Brotherly kindness means to be of a good or benevolent nature. Teach your children to be kind. Kindness is practiced by words, deeds, and thoughts. In the home, practice the art of kindness to each other. I have many memories of kindness shown to me as a child from a loving and kind home. I shall never forget the times I would hear my dear, sweet mother coming to put extra covers on my bed during the night. It was cold and we had no electric blankets, but her kindness made her think of us rather than her own comfort.

Bee Loving: Charity is love. Love uses up-words. The object of our enthusiasm is the benevolent affection of God toward His creation and the reverent affection due to Him from His Creation. Love is also the affectionate concern for the well being of others. In today's society, the general trend is dad and mom both work and the children are either left alone after school or with sitters. My personal belief is that children need at least one of their parents home during these growing years and that siblings were not meant to take care of each other. Who will nurture the good and curb the offensive? These situations usually create the downward spiraling environments which bring children low. Children who are unsupervised can be very cruel and hateful. "I hate you" or "You brat...", etc. should not be used, but if you are not there, who knows what they are saying or how they are behaving?

(See Chapter 2 of our study)

The object of our enthusiasm is the benevolent affection of God toward His creation and the reverent affection due to Him from His Creation.

Developing Talent

Building a Highway for Leadership Character

The very best parent is one who helps a child develop his fullest potential in leadership and talent. It is very simple; your child will follow or lead. You can educate a child, but unless he knows what to do with the information, you have an educated thief. This is why I believe the investments of time, energy, and finance in building leadership characteristics and talents are priceless. In his book, *Nurturing the Leader within Your Child*, author Tim Elmore (2001) points out that talent alone is not sufficient for a balanced child, or we will raise an arrogant, ungrateful generation. The secret lies in balancing character with talent (77). In my years of experience, I have found investments made for talent and leadership have been the golden opportunities for developing character. Practice, self-discipline, and team interaction are all golden, real-life opportunities for teaching and developing character and leadership skills. As a parent, you are building a highway for your child to practice and use leadership character skills. Furthermore, you are building a bridge over the adolescent years of the "Canyon of Despair" (as I like to call it). If you are developing character in your son or daughter, you are well on your way to becoming a winning parent!

Here is a story I thought you would enjoy of one mother who invested time and energy in her son which has paid off in high dividends.

The Little Red Guitar

At age 12, my husband, Royce, pastor of Lighthouse Christian Center, began taking guitar lessons. With money earned from a babysitting job, his mother bought him a beautiful red guitar. With consistent practice, Royce soon played in his home church and later was invited to play in other churches. When he earned the money, he purchased a beautiful red Mosrite guitar, his boyhood dream. This story proves that little seeds, planted and nurtured in our children, may one day grow into great gifts that can be a blessing to everyone. Remember, great oaks come from tiny acorns.

We must first "think" what we would like our children to become and never say it is impossible. Rather, think of one thing they may begin right away to learn. The journey of a thousand miles begins with the first step.

74

Kite Kit Toolbox:
Vocabulary Toolbox for Chapter 3

- Talent
- Recreation
- Motivation
- Skill
- Maximum

- Responsibility
- Arts
- The arts
- Academics
- Minimum

Talent: A gift, a contribution, an award
Recreation: To restore through using time in a hobby, leisure, exercise
Motivation: A stimulating force
Skill: Capability
Maximum: To the fullest degree
Minimum: To the least degree
Responsibility: Accountability
Arts: Activity of creating things
The Arts: Aesthetic beauty, music, paintings, sketches, photography, crafts, and much more
Academics: Pertaining to scholarship

Why Develop Talent?

Developing talent becomes an integral part of the Shine Discipline Plan of Action and serves as a highway for building leadership character.
- Helps parents bond with child
- Helps the parent and child both envision stars to reach
- Helps the child gain positive attention
- Helps the child gain self-control, self-esteem, and teach responsibility through self-discipline which are critical for life (and approaching "Canyon of Despair" - the adolescent years)

How Do I Find My Child's Talents?

Finding your child's talents is like going shopping. Sometimes an item on a shelf may look inviting, until you try it on, and "hands down" the decision is made. It either works or it doesn't. Where do you go shopping for young children's talents? Home, church, and school are the most likely observation balconies.

Your responsibility is to observe them and make wise choices. Talent search is an on-going discovery, and a wise parent begins the journey when their child is only a toddler.

The most likely way to detect talent is to observe your child at interactive play, involve them in Christmas skits, get them involved in church functions, and pay attention to what they enjoy. Many times your child will develop interests in areas the parents themselves enjoy. For instance, how many times do we see musically talented children come from homes where the parents are also musically talented or have a great appreciation for music? Even if you feel you lack in a certain area, the secret to finding your child's talent lies in giving them a potpourri of opportunities. Your responsibility is to observe them and make wise choices. Talent search is an on-going discovery, and a wise parent begins the journey when their child is only a toddler.

The Value of Developing Talent (Self - Esteem)

Most adolescent problems are related to poor self-esteem. A wise parent can head off these problems by helping their child develop their interests and talents early on. Without going into great depth, one can readily see where the involvement of recitals, practices, and just the routine of practices will be a built-in program for self-gratification and will easily build self-esteem. I am not speaking of just music but this would be in any of their interest. For example, if your child's interest is art or photography, get them training early on and display their pictures around the house or frame the best. In addition, most art and photography teachers showcase their students' work once or twice a year in an art or photography show.

One of our parents was especially concerned for their son approaching adolescence and puberty. He seemed to be very insecure, but he covered his insecurity with a very abrasive, independent air. After much prayer and helping this young man become interested in instruments, the parent's struggle began to pay off. Their son's involvement in learning how to play an instrument built up his confidence and self-esteem. He never hit the rocks of puberty but is flying over them with success. His spirit has mellowed and he has become caring and considerate.

Parents are the guides, star miners, seed planters, and nurturers.

What an awesome responsibility to think the destiny of your children lies within your hands. Within each child are innately buried treasures. Parents, as star miners, must search diligently until they find the treasure. Once the treasure is found, the developing process begins until the star is polished and useful to mankind. Unless we come to the stark reality that it is our responsibility to find a talent, how can we manage to do the next step of developing it? Yes, God is ultimately the author and finisher of our lives, but, as parents, it is up to us to furnish our children's suitcase for the future. We must pray diligently for God's guidance; and when we see natural seeds that were planted by God displayed in our child's desires, then as your child's guide, act upon it. Start nurturing what God has planted in their hearts.

The Little Blue Accordion

I remember as a little girl, about 9 years old, not being particularly old enough to understand all that was taking place at church. However, I had a love for music which my parents nurtured by giving me piano lessons. I was given the opportunity to play at a very early age for it was a relatively small congregation.

When I was about 12 years old, I was intrigued by a beautiful blue accordion. Coming from a large family, I had no idea that one day I would ever have my very own. But a little girl's dream did come true and the best Christmas I remember was the Christmas I received a gorgeous blue accordion.

That summer, after receiving the accordion, I was scheduled to go to Houston, Texas, for a scoliosis surgery. Deep down inside, I carried a little seed in my mind and heart that one day I would play the blue accordion. This desire went with me through the many struggles of rod-infusion surgery and recovery with all of its complications, such as lying flat on my back for six months, wearing a body cast, and dealing with the battle of the bed pan. Now that I look back, my embarrassment was nothing compared to my mothers and sister's task of taking care of me.

After many more stories that are too numerous for now, the day did come when the little seed of playing my accordion became a reality. What humorous childhood memories, as this little 12 year old made happy sounds to her first captive audience, the cows grazing in the meadows nearby. However, I must blink back happy tears even now as I recall these days when, no doubt, I was learning the sweet presence of my forever friend, Jesus.

Later, the day arrived when I received a more state-of-the-art accordion from my husband, Royce, which I still have as an engagement present.

Today, church and my love for helping others is a way of life. Did someone's nurturing a desire for music in my life help me to love church? The answer would have to be, yes. There are back doors where we must look to plant seeds in the direction we would like our children to develop. I am thankful for my parents who planted the seeds of music in my life and helped me use it in a positive direction.

With nurture, little seeds grow and little dreams come true.

Although music is only one of the many areas where children can develop talent, it is an excellent way to nurture seeds of going to church.

N
W ← ○ → E
S

The idea is to get tough on yourself by selecting a talent to develop in your child's life. Remember, developing your child's gifts brings out self-esteem and creates a good base to start character building for the road to leadership.

Setting the Compass
"The value of choosing the correct talents"

My daughter and I were driving up the highway on US 95 when she announced, "You made a wrong turn! "With exasperation, she went on to let me know that my mistake may cause me to miss the 1 o'clock plane I was try-ing to catch. The whole trip would soon be in vain if I did not quickly correct my course.

Many people make wrong turns in life and never take the time to get back on track. Being off track causes them to miss the big picture for their life, their fam-ily, and their children. Why waste your energy in putting yourself through the regiment and expense of something if you are missing your big picture? Which bend do you want your child to have? Do you want them to have a bend toward wanting to go to church? Then help them develop a talent where they can be useful in church. What is wrong with that? You may say, "Well, I want them to ride horses or join the wrestling team." Well, that may make a good recreation for a season, but where will it lead? If you were going to the state of Florida and you lived in the East, you would set your compass South. If you give poor calls as a guide, you may find yourself in a different place than you dreamed.

Check your compass, map, and time clock. How much time do you have? To discover and develop talents that are in check with your big-picture, values cannot be over stressed. Every child is going to seek attention from the steady knocking on his desk, to clown acts – these will result in negative attention. We need parents who accept the responsibility to find ways to help their child develop a positive way to receive attention.

Positive is the key word here. It cannot be a negative outcome in your evalu-ations above and still be positive. For example, if your child likes horseback rid-ing, playing ball, creating music, etc., will the types of activities that go along with his choice fulfill your big-picture goal for your family? For instance, if spiritual relationship is a priority, what will happen when the activity does not lead to Sunday church? With what kind of peer group will your child intermingle as they pursue their interest? Wise parents take a hard look at the door where they are leading their children. After all, when our child does not end up where we intended, we will be responsible. The idea is to get tough on yourself by select-ing a talent to develop in your child's life. Remember, developing your child's gifts brings out self-esteem and creates a good base to start character building for the road to leadership. The statistics are in your favor, so watch for the "shine" as you search for a talent to bring out the best in your child.

Talents vs. Sports

Some families confuse developing a child's talent with sports. While it may take talent to achieve in sports, you will not produce the same character/leadership skills as involvement in music, speech, drama, crafts, sewing, art, photography, etc. Each child is uniquely designed with talent traits that appear naturally God-given. For example, some children develop their speech centers at an early age and talk non-stop. By early observation, if this child is consistently rooted in an environment that nurtures singing, reading, drama, and other linguistic exercises, they will no doubt be gifted toward public speaking and singing. You cannot plant potatoes and produce tomatoes. Some sports take particular talent, such as focusing on a goal; however, you will not be enhancing literary skills. So, while your child is actively involved and spending hours developing competitive and goal oriented skills, your child may not want to make speeches in the youth group. He would probably love to interact with a group playing ball, but you have to ask yourself what you are trying to build? While a child may love horses, will caring for the horse, riding practices, and the overall picture fit into your lifestyle? Is this what you want for your child? If literary goals are a top priority, you need to find an area to build. You must think of how much time you are giving to the matter and if this is what you want in their life. After much research, I believe sports make a good recreation but should not be substituted for literary study or arts development.

Recreation

The definition of recreation means to restore. This definition alone suggest that if we fulfull its meaning we will restore. In our case, it means restore our health and bodies. Every family should find ways to enjoy recreation together. Whatever you enjoy, in a healthy sense, can be recreation. This is where sports can enter in the picture (swimming, ball-playing, fishing, walking, hiking, or other relaxing activities). Balancing recreation along with developing talent and character is the key to good parenting.

Sports

Many times children will gravitate to sports and sometimes this seems to be an area where they are particularly gifted. Use this gift as one of your Door's of Life incentive plan, but make sure you require academic achievement and talent development in other areas. Balancing recreation along with developing talent, academics, and character is the key to good parenting.

After much research, I believe sports make a good recreation but should not be substituted for literary study or arts development.

Bee An Encourager

"If my mother and father think I can do it, it doesn't matter what anybody else thinks; I know I can do it." This is the way I thought and I believe it is the way most kids think. Find something your child does well. It could be just sitting still a few minutes. Tell him how nice and quiet he is. Perhaps he is nice to a pet. Tell him you liked the way he treated the animal. Just keep looking and encouraging. You'll have a winner. A word of encouragement is like a ton of fertilizer, it is like Miracle-Gro. Just keep pouring it on and your plants will flourish and the up-words will cause your parenting kite to fly high.

Star Talk ☆

What star do you want to catch?

Don't get hung up on hang-ups. Hang ups are the negative outcomes when parents choose the wrong talent to develop or the wrong fun thing to do.

Remember standing on High Hopes Hill with your spouse? Did you count what you desired in your children's life in terms of retaining character and moral values? It is not time to waver but time to stand firm on your value system.

Check Out the Value System... How much does it cost?

This chapter is speaking on developing talents, but keep in mind that everything we do should be done with the motive of instilling the values of God and family into our children's lives. For instance, what kind of music we allow our child to hear, what kind of environment we allow our children to be around, what kinds of DVDs and videos we allow them to watch, what kind of computer games we allow them to play, what sports interests we allow them to pursue, what kind of literary achievements we expect them to achieve, etc., will have an effect on the person they will become. This is where the big picture must come into the forefront.

Kite Talent Search

Questions to ask about the value system surrounding a particular interest:

- Is the involvement in connection to the Word of God?
- Is it right individually for my child, or is it something that I always wanted?
- What kind of environment and people will be there?
- What kind of clothing will it require?
- What will be the ultimate and total outcome of the skill, involvement, or participation?
- Is participation risky to life and limb?

- Is it worth it for a thrill?
- By allowing them to participate, am I bending the bow that may set his direction?
- Will participation make them a better person?
- Does the crowd he is around smoke? drink? use foul language?
- It is known children become what they are around. Is this what you want your child to become?

After you have evaluated the questions above and there is agreement between child and parents, then you are ready to begin your talent quest.

Musical Talents

Age-appropriate music development can begin as early as 2-8 years of age by having them be involved with music programs at church or in school. Special music schools exist that provide music appreciation programs for toddlers. The main thing is to be careful not to start lessons so early that their attention span and responsibility level will produce inconsistent practice times, especially when learning to play an instrument. Band instruments need special care so age is another point of consideration. According to a local instrument advisor, the age of 8 or 9 is a good time to start band lessons.   Piano lessons may begin earlier. That again has to do with a parent's decision to invest financially and the child's practice abilities.

Vocal Talents

Singing is one talent all children should have the opportunity to discover. The market is full of karaoke tape players of all qualities and styles. Investments made in sound tracks and other instrumental means gives them the opportunity to have their own concerts starting at home under their own spot lights and stage. It can be a fun way to entertain guests and loved ones in a positive way. Of course, children should be singing in church and school by way of consistent involvement.

Achievement Days

Achievement days at school may be another way to discover a skill or talent hidden in a child. Some children love to study science, let them have at it! Some children love to write stories or poems. Encourage them! Below is a list of suggestions. Remember, there should never be a boring day at your house if you keep a list of suggestions nearby.

On dark nights when you are lonely... stars always shine brighter...

If Your Child Has Extra Time, What Would He Rather Do?
- Arts, pencil, oil, acrylic, water-color
- Music, string, wind, percussion
- Vocal, solo, karaoke
- Literary, academics, reading, vocal reading
- Storytelling
- Puppetry
- Sports activities
- Dramatics
- Science projects
- Computer skills
- Photography
- Journaling
- Bible Quizzing

A Place To Land the "Shine" (See appendix for 150 suggestions to "Shine")

Nothing motivates like knowing there is a place you can land your shine. A child who practices daily on a sax but only plays for his mother or dad, may lose a certain fizz for his practice. However, if he knows he is going to cheer the elderly or perform in a city affair, his spirits will rise. Participation in community functions, volunteer cheer groups, or church and school events offers a few of the landing strips.

Star Talk ☆

Give children a positive way to shine. Build character and self esteem.

A child needs a place to shine. Increase their self-esteem by giving them opportunities to shine in front of an audience and encourage them to give their talent to the Lord. Areas of service where your child can give back his talent to the Lord are nursing homes, day cares, churches, schools, and community services. The way to get in the loop of any of the above is to get connected with an information service within these facilities. For many of these groups, just becoming a member and being faithful will automatically give you and your child a place to serve. There are many places where there are lonely people, and your child could be a blessing. Start today to help your child find their talent and to give it back as a service to the Lord.

Shining Star character traits are achieved by giving talent back to God through service to the community, church, and family. The investments you make into your children's lives will pay great dividends through puberty's rough days that could leave you angry and frustrated. Instead, your joy will overflow for your star will be found shining, giving of himself, and cheering the world!

In the next few pages, it is my desire to help us see our children in a new light.

Academic Learning Styles

In this section, we want to think about the way your child learns. Does a child have to sit in rows of chairs with a chalkboard in front of him to learn?

Education, the cornerstone for advancement, has also enjoyed progress by the use of a new system unlocking how you learn. In 1967, Rita and Kenneth Dunn showed through multiple research the importance of applying a new layer to the profile of how we learn, called Learning Styles. For people like me and perhaps yourself, it is exciting to know there are more ways than one to measure a person's intelligence than the traditional IQ Test. While this is not meant to be an in-depth study of the subject, it is meant to turn the light on for a new way to think when it comes to dealing with your child and his school work. If you are one of the parents who have struggled with helping Susie do her homework assignment or motivating Johnny to read, the next few pages could be of utmost value for you.

Cynthia Tobias (1996), CEO of Apple St. Academic Learning Styles of Seattle, Washington, made a great study of how children learn in her book entitled, *Every Child Can Succeed*. Tobias says of the growing attention deficit disorder epidemic, "They all can't have ADD" (103). While I am not doing an in-depth study on ADD (Attention Deficit Disorder), I do think it very important to mention I highly recommend her books for your study. So many times, children are labeled ADD and some doctors and educators alike are wondering if ADD really exists at all. Thomas Armstrong, an outstanding educator and popular author, asks, "I wonder whether this 'disorder' really exists in the child at all, or whether, more properly it exists in the relationships that are present between the child and his/her environment. Unlike other medical disorders, such as diabetes or pneumonia, this is a disorder that pops up in one setting only to disappear in another." This author like many others, is very concerned because the Ritalin medication used to treat ADD has been proven to trigger Tourette's Syndrome, an incurable disease that is characterized by uncontrollable motor/verbal movements.

Another early observation parents should watch for could be hearing or visual problems. A continuation of turning a letter backwards could indicate visual problems or it could indicate dyslexia. Two types of dyslexia are auditory and visual. Sometimes it is difficult to diagnose children early on, but the earlier they are diagnosed, the sooner treatment can be administered. Much progress has been made in the reatment of dyslexia and most

They all can't have ADD.
Cynthia Tobias

83

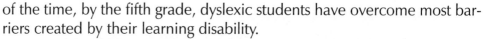

of the time, by the fifth grade, dyslexic students have overcome most barriers created by their learning disability.

Our goal for this study is to turn the motor on within your child, turning on the "want to." Our goal is to help you find the key to unlock your child's style for a happier and richer life. Horizons of research have been done on the subject of learning styles, and what I give to you is an introduction to help take away some fears many people suffer from thinking they or their children may not be as smart as someone else. Every one can shine somewhere and one of the core factors, according to many researchers, is finding the child's learning style.

The following list is a brief overview of learning styles. You will probably find your learning style somewhere in the picture as well as that of your child. Remember, it is never a clear-cut picture, rather a blend with a dominance of two styles. At the end of this chapter, you will be asked to build a word index for your child. The word index will help you know your child better, who he is, what he enjoys most, the time of the day he does his work best, what his personality style is, and more.

Styles To Consider:
- Auditory: Works through a thought process verbally.
- Visual: Captures ideas from charts and illustrations.
- Kinesthetic: Animated and learns best through physical activity and energy.
- Analytic: Works better if he knows the details.
- Global: Sees and understands the big picture.
- Abstract--Sequential: Likes working with facts (e.g., documentaries)
- Concrete --Sequential: Loves to organize and detail work.
- Abstract--Random: Has a deep sense of other's needs and feelings; peacemakers. They are also spontaneous, flexible, and love to give gifts.

Ben Carson: Who Said He Was Dumb?

Ben Carson would have never been Dr.Ben Carson if his mother would have accepted their plight in life. She had come from a family of twenty-four children, and at the age of 13, married having only a 3rd grade education. She could not even read her children's papers to see if they were right, but one thing she knew; if they were going to triumph over their poverty, they had to have an education. She insisted her boys not watch TV but do their reports. Even though she could not read, she would have the boys read their reports to her.

Early on, one of Ben Carson's teachers had labeled him as the dumb kid. Sure enough, he never seemed to catch on. However, that didn't stop his mother. She put it in him that he was as smart as the next one, and he believed her. Even after being accepted into Yale University and then going to Michigan Medical School, he hit another hard bump. Another teacher said, "Why don't you take four years to complete what most people do in two?" Ben determined not to take the ghetto mind-set, for he knew he learned better by reading not hearing lectures. No wonder he was having difficulties, for most of his classes were communicated through lecture. Ben turned to his best learning style, which was reading, and the rest is history.

Dr. Ben Carson, world renowned brain surgeon, now says, "A victim walking through sand looks down and sees dirt; a victor looks down and sees material for building a castle." Who said that boy was dumb? Thank God for a mother who wouldn't take no for an answer and a boy who believed her.

Thank God for a mother who wouldn't take no for an answer and a boy who believed her.

Time Management

In Ephesians 5:15 - 6:18, Paul admonishes us to be careful to spend our time wisely. Wisely, in terms of parenting, purpose should be the most valuable priority. This brings us back to view our "Big Picture" parenting purpose. Although it is a reminder of the various things we need to do, it also serves as a reminder to keep our parenting purpose foremost in priority.

Time managers are not born, they are developed. It is a life-long process.

Applying Wisdom to our Time Management

God	Worship time at church... and private devotions
Family	Fulfilling needs of mate, children (basic four areas)
Job	Time designated for earning a living
Miscellaneous	Managing finances, household work, friends, services

Time Management for Parents

Now that you are working on your child's character and talent development and are busy helping them develop their academics, time is the next element you must help them manage. It was not the fast rabbit that won the race but the consistent tortoise. Consistency is the word which needs to be stressed in the life of a shining Star. Managing time can be taught

through a variety of ways.

Some parents use a daily record, keeping it on the refrigerator for easy reference-at-a-glance. The record should show practice schedules and use some method of tracking time spent on tasks as well as measuring progress and achievement. Every effort a child makes equals a reward of some sort. The main idea is to strive toward a reward system that not only encourages independence for your child but at the same time, offers the parent a quick way to check their progress at a glance. A built-in reward system is always the best. For example, smaller children may use the happy basket and get a ticket, which might mean going outside for play-time, a treat at the store, or a favorite sticker. The sad basket gives sad tickets which may mean time out or you don't get to go outside and play. The appendix has a goal chart and a time pie-chart that you can copy for your own family's use if you so desire.

(Sample) Family Shine Time Schedule

- 6:30 – Rise and shine, wash up and get dressed
- 7:00 – Breakfast
- 7:20 – Daily devotion, prayer and Bible reading
- 7:30 – Children make beds, morning routine, and brush teeth
- 8:00 – Children leave for school
- 3:30 – Children return home; free time - relax
- 4:00 – Practice instrument or talent skill
- 4:30 – Start homework, study, etc
- 5:00 – Dinner
- 5:45 – Do a few chores
- 6:30 – Finish any unfinished task
- 7:00 – Toddlers through five years start on night's routine – bath time, story time, etc. 6-8 years or older children may enjoy time with friends, family, or have fun; also good time to work on extra curricular subjects.

Saturdays and Sundays include a different time management. Make sure you mark Sunday for God. Many parents find it helpful to use Saturday evenings to prepare for Sunday activity. Games, movies (if allowed), and everything can be prepared ahead to truly make this a day reserved for spiritual growth. Remember you will be the winner.

Sample Family Clock

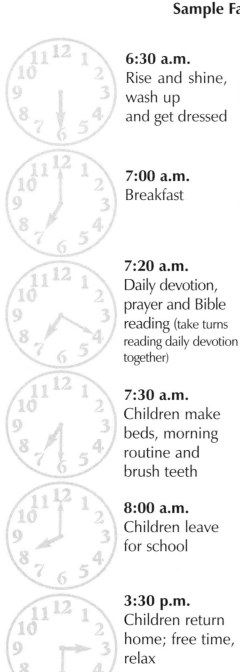

6:30 a.m.
Rise and shine,
wash up
and get dressed

7:00 a.m.
Breakfast

7:20 a.m.
Daily devotion,
prayer and Bible
reading (take turns
reading daily devotion
together)

7:30 a.m.
Children make
beds, morning
routine and
brush teeth

8:00 a.m.
Children leave
for school

3:30 p.m.
Children return
home; free time,
relax

4:00 p.m.
Practice
instrument or
talent skill

4:30 p.m.
Start homework,
study, etc.

5:00 p.m.
Dinner

5:45 p.m.
Do a few chores

6:30 p.m.
Finish any
unfinished task

7:00 p.m.
Toddlers through
five years start on
nights routine -
story down time.
6-8 year olds can have
special time with family
and friends or extra cur-
ricular activities.

A nightly tuck-in with a story that teaches a moral and a prayer is a good way to close the day for your child. Giving your children a hug and gently tucking them in bed tells them you love them. Praying nightly with your child helps them understand that God is real and that there is someone bigger than themselves and bigger than mom and dad. Soon they will be able to pray by themselves.

Teens enjoy their time with you individually, too. Reading good short stories or biblical passages together keeps the bonding in place. This gives you a connecting time if your teen needs to talk. Try arranging taking turns with children for special nights. These special moments make extra time for enjoying special coffees or drinks together, but most of all memories.

Star Talk ☆

Consistency is the word which needs to be stressed in good time management of shining Stars.

Tools for Time Chart
- Schedule- a plan, timetable, a program
- Consistency- certainty, routinely, accountable
- Habits- and Routines –to be in a rut
- Focus- concentrate, central
- Goal- aim, objective
- Personalized Calendar- a particular calendar with markings for your needs
- Palm Pilot- a small modern new technical calendar that fits in your hand
- Charts- markings to help you or your child reach your goal: monthly, daily, or weekly

Official Bee-liever's
Certificate of Authenticity
Member of the Bee Family

"I am better than a bumblebee"
I Bee- Lieve I CAN FLY!
This certificate, hereby certifies that,

(Parent's name) _____

agrees to the following:

_____

I _____ , agree that as of today

_____ (date), the parents of, _____ ,

_____ and _____ ,

agree to do as much as the bumblebee and overcome anything that
will keep me out of the air.

I agree to find at least one thing my child does well and promote his practice time

_____ , and day by day he will grow self-esteem.

He will grow character for I agree to train him in a particular life lesson such as

one hour on _____ each week.

His/Her self-esteem will flourish!

Signed _____

(kite flyer)

I am better than the bee!
This bee certificate is good for growing flyers, any shape, size, or color.
My child will grow in these areas - character, talent, and academics.
My pledge as a Bee Parent is to Bee there, to bee a model Bee, and Bee-lieve in my child.
I promise to bee a provider helping him/her to bee productive!

Kite Talk:
Evaluation for Chapter 3

In this chapter, we discussed developing

Your child's _____ , _____ , _____ ,

by using the _____ plan. The "Shine" plan motivates by using

_____ and _____ which unlocks the door to

_____ skills in your child.

1.   What thought helped the Bumblebee to fly?

_____

2.   Can you name the fruits of the Spirit that every Bee-lieving
       family should have?

_____

3.   "Setting my child up to BEE a winner" -- Work out your sam-
       ple model of the Shine Action Plan 1, 2, 3 for your child.

_____

4.   Why is developing talent an important job for parents?

_____

5.   What are some time management priorities in your life?

_____

6.   What are some tools for keeping track of time and achieve-
       ment?

_____

Notes

_____

_____

_____

_____

_____

_____

_____

_____

_____

Chapter 4

RAISING KITES AND KIDS

DISCIPLINING TECHNIQUES,
"SHINE" DISCIPLINING PLAN,
AND PARENTING STYLES

CHAPTER 4

93

Chapter 4

RAISING KITES AND KIDS

DISCIPLINING TECHNIQUES, "SHINE" DISCIPLINING PLAN, AND PARENTING STYLES

Discipline Hedges

Discipline is the art of building hedges and security which really begins in the womb. When a mother limits her choice of consumption of things such as alcohol and drugs, and does not eat foods that upset her, she is protecting her baby and already building hedges for his well being. As you read the chart below, keep in mind that the first seven years in a child's life are the most critical years because this is the time when personality is created and blends are being made that will affect the child for the rest of his life. Especially during this time frame, children need discipline in the form of safety, hedges, and routines in order for them to develop properly.

> "The hand that rocks the cradle and shapes the nation is disappearing; ironically, so is the moral fabric of the nation."

Safety, Hedges, and Routines

Techniques in nurturing and training for the very young child allow parents to keep their grip on the string.

Age	0-1	2-3	4-5	6-7
Molding and Shaping Temperament And Personality	Security: A child's basic security is gathered by their ability to decipher sensations and plan actions	Meal time should be pleasant: with healthy routines	Challenges of eating. BE CONSISTENT. Be firm, yet kind	Use meal time for practicing good manners and positive self-image. However, if correction needs to take place, try to play it down and do it at a different time

> Is the child training you or are you training the child?

95

Age	0-1	2-3	4-5	6-7
Nutrition - Start as early as 2 weeks; start placing a soft spoon on baby's tongue to help them get used to the feel. Some have found this training allows for spoon feedings as early as 3-4 weeks and helps transition	Routine feeding is the key… Wait at least 3-4 hrs. (too soon and baby will not eat or get satisfied) toy distractions and making noises helps baby eat.	Allow child to hold spoon as soon as he tries… keep encouraging. However, finger foods, chicken sticks, and fruit snacks are favorites at this age.	Finicky eaters can be handled by saying, "Okay, if you do not want to eat your chicken sticks and you want snacks, that is fine. However, here is your chicken (etc.) when you decide to eat this, then you can have your snack."	Using this time to play games such as describing picture cards. It could be a box of cards on table.
Changing Clothing Choosing etc.	When changing baby clothes or diaper, especially as they get older, hold the child's leg firmly and let them know you are in control. Do not allow running from you when changing diaper	Potty training can be done as early as child begins to walk and begins using a cup. There are videos and books on this subject. Stickers and awards are fun.	If your child is one that likes to choose his clothes, that is okay, but limit his choices. Place two shirts on the bed and let him choose between those articles.	Using this time to play games such as describing picture cards. It could be a box of cards on table.
Bathing Bedtime etc.		Children need space and time. As you allow them to bathe, use this time to prepare their minds for bedtime by saying, "When you finish your bath, we will have our story," or say, "It's nightime."		

Training:
Diaper Changes:
  Diaper changes are a good way to teach your child boundaries or hedges early on. Firmly holding the infant's leg while you are changing the diaper lets them know their limits. This way they feel safe but also know exactly what the boundaries are.

Spoon Feedings:
  Spoon feedings are important for healthy, happy babies. Start perhaps with touching the spoon to his tongue (at least within 6 weeks). Touching the spoon to the tongue around 6 weeks is necessary especially for extra sensitive temperaments. Many physicians differ in their advice to parents about the time to begin spoon feedings, but as a parent, you must get to know your baby and understand their temperament. If he is sensitive, touching the tongue with a spoon early on is very important: otherwise, he may not be willing to eat from a spoon until he is around five years old.

Sleep Routines:
  Letting children know who is in charge begins at infancy. I believe in a motto I once heard, "You can train the child or they will train you." You may read and hear all kinds of advice about feedings and sleep patterns. In general, a good rule of thumb is to wait long enough between feedings. Otherwise, a baby will nibble small amounts just long enough to fall back into a short nap. You will be the trainer by taking charge and deciding how long the intervals of time should be before the next feeding. (This will be especially appreciated at night with the longer intervals of rest.) You don't have to hold a lion's whip over your child to accomplish this. Just continually follow a schedule and keep your routines consistent.

  As your children grow older, rituals communicate time. For example, to help during bedtime rituals, you may use a favorite story, place a guiding hand on the shoulder or give a warning "30 more minutes" (even if they don't know what 30 minutes means). These simple bedtime rituals are signals that prepare the child's mind for change. Preparation signals are especially important for children with sensitive temperaments. In short, consistency of routines improves a child's general mood and also helps their sleep patterns.

Star Talk ☆

Setting routines in the early years of a baby's life should be thought of not just as bottle time or bed time, etc., but should be thought of, instead, with deep sincerity, for no doubt the structure you as the parent set is the beginning of the way you will treat them the rest of their life. Researchers have found that most juvenile delinquents come from domestically violent homes which did not have stability early on in their lives. According to statistics presented from Heritage (see Chapter 1), I was astonished to see that most of these children had no patterns or hedges. This went on to follow them into school, where they were labeled the attention deficit ones and given medicine inconsistently which led to other complications. This mind-boggling information hopefully will increase your desire and appreciation for consistently training and disciplining your child.

Researchers have found that most juvenile delinquents come from domestically violent homes and did not have stability early on in their lives.

Kite Kit Toolbox:

Vocabulary Toolbox for Chapter 4
Understanding Discipline

· Obedience
· Respect
· Open Defiance
· Forgetfulness
· Courteousness
· Unacceptable Behavior

· Train
· Discipline
· Parenting Styles
· Disciplining Techniques

Respect: Esteem, admiration, the condition of being honored
Open Defiance: When a child openly challenges authority or shows resistance to authority by actions that are deliberate and disrespectful. Open defiance can be shown through body language, facial expression, or verbal challenge. This type of disobedience calls for an immediate form of discipline.
Forgetfulness: Not remembering is a normal characteristic of growing children. However, positive and negative reminders help nurture responsible development. You can deal with a sweater being left at school every once in a while: but when it becomes an everyday occurrence, you must enact measures that will help the child remember.
Courteousness: Kindness - Children should be taught to be courteous. They should be taught to look a person in the eye when speaking or being spoken to. Children should be taught that elderly people are very special to God, and they should not bump into them or be unkind. They should remember to say, "Excuse me, please" and practice daily habits of courteous gestures. Children who have good manners go a long way in life, but manners are learned behavior and must be taught, not left to chance.

Unacceptable Behavior: This is the term used when speaking to your children about behavior which you do not allow.
Train: To instruct, bring up or condition; to guide the mental, moral, spiritual development of your child.
Discipline: Training which results in the development of self-control and character.
Parenting Styles: The style of Parenting or taking care of children.
Authoritative - Henry the Hurler   Balanced Parenting - Heidi the High flyer;
Manipulative - Fiber optic   Unstable - Wandering Star
Disciplining Techniques: Techniques used to bring about a favorable action.
Shine, Cueing, Isolation, Hebrew, Report Writing

Star Wheel
For Nurturing Physical, Emotional (Spiritual), Mental, and Social Hedges

Emotional Hedge
· Builds security and love
· Be affectionate, gentle
· Star cup filled.
· Be dependable
· Use up-words that encourage and support
· Start day and finish day with special moments
· Teach values and model consistency.
· Be affectionate especially when your child is hurt physically or emotionally

Mental Hedge
· Provide activities
· Education, positive lifestyle and environment for healthy growth and stability
· Discover your child's temperament and learning style

Time Hedge
· Look for and develop talent
· Build routines for security
· Find your child by finding what he does well and develop it by using "Next Door Growth"
· Celebrate your child's life with your time investments
· Include his friends

Physical Hedge
· Provide food, shelter, clothing
· Teach hygiene
· Provide medical care and regular health exams
· Eye glasses
· Dental
· Braces by 7 or 9

Star Shine
Instilling Spiritual Values
· **S**tand on Values
· **T**ogether build relationships
· **A**, B, C's of communications
· **A**bilities: find your child by discovering talents, mental style of learning, and temperament
· **R**esponsible, respectful discipline; find your parenting style
· Teach consequential behavior; mean what you say and evaluate it before you say it. By age 2, children should obey simple commands such as sit, stand, come, stay, etc.
· **S** - Shine; envisioning who they are and can become is more important than good grades.
· Shine... Parents Mapping Zone
· Evaluate Priorities

Disciplining Techniques:

The Kite String

As in the illustration of the kite, the string is the guiding force that is comparable to disciplining or training a child. For example, if you give the kite too much string, it will become limp and fall; but if you don't give it enough string, it will pull away from your hand and not go up. There is definitely an art in knowing when to give more string and when to pull back. Although the challenge keeps even the best of kite flyers on their toes, we know there are many skilled kite flyers who can keep the kite rising and stable against the forces of the wind.

Parenting Secrets - Window of Time for Molding: (More secrets in the 6th chapter)
1. It is important to listen carefully and act quickly on wrong traits (don't wait until they become habits). Dr. Dobson's book, *Parenting Isn't For Cowards,* shows the importance of acting quickly on whiney or negative dispositions, facial expressions, etc. He reminds parents that the formula of love and discipline has been tested and validated over many centuries of time. It can work for you too.

2. However, disciplining must begin early while a child's will is still moldable. I love the point Dr. Dobson shares about the importance of time. He states, "A child only has a small window of opportunity" (355). Dr. Dobson goes on to compare the larynx of a young child to the importance of shaping his will. Have you ever wondered why it is so easy to teach languages to children without even a trace of an accent? According to Dr. Dobson, researchers now know why this is true. It is explained by a process known as "phoneme contraction" (sound dropout). The larynx of a young child assumes a shape necessary to make the sound he is learning to use at the time. It then solidifies or hardens into those positions, making it impossible or very difficult to make other sounds later in life. Thus, there is a brief window of opportunity where anything is possible linguistically: But that **window of time** doesn't last forever. It will soon be history.

3. Molding a child's attitude toward parental authority is also like that. He passes through a brief window of opportunity during late infancy and toddlerhood where respect and awe for parental authoirty can be instilled. But that pliability will not last long. If his early reach for power is successful, he will not willingly give it up - ever. A spanking should be reserved and occur in response to willful defiance. Period! This discipline is not recommended to be used as a last resort, but intended for defiant behavior whenever it is needed (355).

4. Parents should always evaluate situations and ask themselves why their child is out of order or misbehaving. In my experience, I found I had to do less disciplining or restraining measures if I listened to the child more carefully and set aside special time alone with that particular child. It is very hard to do this, but dealing with certain negative traits immediately instead of tolerating them until they fester full blown is a very important secret in child rearing. **It is a secret for it seems many parents do not know this.** Parents should evaluate the role their personality plays in their child's behavior and also evaluate their parenting style and ask themselves whether they are being consistent in training their child and not sending mixed messages. When discipline is necessary, realize there is more than one option.

Disciplining Techniques

While there are many different techniques of discipline, we will discuss the following five:

- · Isolation
- · Reasoning
- · Cueing
- · Hebrew style of corporal discipline and love
- · Consequential and report writing

As one school of thought puts it, there is not a one cure-all method of discipline for children. Children come in different shapes, temperaments, and needs. I have never found the e-z pass, one-ticket, cure-all for this disciplining journey. Of all the studies and real life experiences, I have found life makes its own currency and what works one time may not always work the next or for someone else. The five methods of discipline are meant to be used in different situations and under different circumstances. In other words, all these methods work well, but please keep in mind that different circumstances and different children require different methods of discipline.

The Isolation Method

One method of disciplining children is the counting and isolation method. In this method, after so many counts the child will go to a designated place of isolation such as a bedroom, special chair, etc. away from everyone else. While this may seem to work at times, it is not a cure-all. I have known children who are left alone after an offense to sometimes becomes violent, withdrawn, and overly aggressive. However, in some cases, some authors believe isolation with other measures can bring a child and home back into order.

101

I have seen it work in some cases when a child was ruling his house by his tantrums and throwing things. For example, Jack was seven years old and had ruled his younger brother and mother by yelling and aggressive behavior. When his dad got home, Jack gave him no peace by jumping on him and vehemently demanding his attention. After seeking professional help, the doctor suggested the child was over-stimulated and the parents were advised to remove all of his toys, which were too many, plus his personal T.V. Only a bed was left in his room. He had to earn back his toys and other rights by correct behavior. During this time, no whining was allowed, no throwing things, no demanding rights. He had to ask for special prizes, not demand them. He also had to ask for attention. Nor was he allowed to jump on his dad when he came home from work. Slowly Jack lost the power he held by behaving wrong. In time, his behavior became more tolerable.

The Reasoning Method

This philosophy encourages parents to reason with children about their unacceptable behavior. While reasoning may have its positive effects at an appropriate age level, have you ever seen a mother reasoning with a little 3 year old about sticking his tongue out at adults? For example, Anna, late for work, drops her 3-year-old, Sheila, off to nursery school. As she kisses her daughter good-bye, she sees Sheila sticking her tongue out at her teacher. Should she run back into the car with her? If she did that she would be late for work. When Anna finally coaxed her daughter to apologize to her teacher, Sheila began throwing a tantrum and tried to bite when Anna tried to stop her. The next step would be explaining to Sheila that children don't bite and kick. The only problem was that Sheila couldn't hear her mother talking because her behavior had escalated to screaming. By now, Mommy knew Sheila had won. The popular teaching of letting the child express themselves was doing wonders for Sheila's expression, but not much in the line of taming her wild spirit. Anna had to toss reason out the window; the only solution was to remove Sheila from the room until she calmed down.

The Cueing Method (age appropriate)

In order for the cueing method to work, a child must be an active listener and careful watcher. It is essential that a child learn to be attentive to the parent for this discipline-warning system to work. When a one-year old knows what 'no' and 'yes' means, it is time to incorporate signals to reinforce correct behavior.

If a parent does this with a firm tap to the inside portion of the hand or to the bottom consistently and continues to have other areas in sync, the child will learn he is not in charge. In my opinion, the cueing method shows very good parenting, for at a very young age the child learns to be compliant to the parent. For instance, one parent reported:

 My child, Mona, who had a sanguine-phlegmatic personality trait, responded so well to gentle tapings on the palm. Just a stern look was all it took for her to comply all throughout her life. We loved her too much to give her an inconsistent messages. Around ten months old, my oldest daughter Mona, was in her walker. At that time walkers were popular, and hers looked like a space shuttle. I had plastic, decorative grapes out on a shelf, and wanted to teach her never to pick them up, because I knew they might choke her. One day the inevitable happened. She took off in her space shuttle to discover the grapes, and of course I spied her. True to my conviction, I looked at her and shook my head no and said, "No, no, no". And she backed away. Coming out of another room was an aunt, who evaluated the scenario from a different perspective. When I went out of the room, my sister gave the grape to her. As it turned out, the next time I put her in the space shuttle, she headed for the grapes. The confused message, made her unsure of her action. However, as she picked up the grape, a tap on her hand and a "no" reassured her of the correct behavior. Almost from that time, anytime I said "NO", because she believed me, she would not do it.

This same parent has three more children, each have different personalities. Bearing in mind the parental age and experience, along with child-birth order, each child's response to correction was different. For some it took more than one or two messages, but in each case by the time they were five, most of their corporal training was over. That was the good news for this mother.

Dr. Dobson reaffirms this philosophy in his book, *The Strong Willed Child*. Parents, who begin disciplining their children when they are very young can implement warning signals and cues with ease later when the child is older and attentive, making their lives so much easier. In his book, *Making Children Mind Without Losing Yours*, Dr. Leman agrees spanking is an option but warns parents to always be sure you are doing it as loving correction (93). Another author calls this phenomenon "levels of obedience", and suggests that by age two, children should be at an animal level of obedience. Although, I was abhorred by the comparison to an animal, I had to agree that some animals are trained in their skills to sit, come, lay down, etc. much better than some children at age two. Why is that true? What is happening? Can parents no longer get a grip on their children? The old saying, "The hand that rocks the cradle shapes the nation." Ironically the hand that rocks the cradle is disappearing and so is the moral fiber in the nation.

Obeying the "First Time", Using the Smile Game
(Catching the attitude before it becomes a habit)

In our home we practiced what we called listening to Mom or Dad's calling the first time with a smile. The first time I said, "Come here," I expected the child to come. This training starts when they are old enough to understand 'no', and 'yes'. IT IS VERY HARD ON THE PARENT, BUT IT MAKES IT WONDERFUL LATER. Usually around 12 months a child understands simple commands. If they act like they cannot hear, and you know they did, little tappings can assure them you mean business. For the first two to three years in their life, it is as if you are their constant breath, for you are looking for attitudes, gestures of eyes, of the mouth and any tell tale signs of disobedience. Tapping in on these cues early saves you grief and helps the child not to harm himself. No tolerance for even a tell-tale attitude sign is hard work on parents, but it is better to do it when they are two than have grief for the next twenty years and more.

If you see children well behaved and sitting still in church or other public places, it is because someone has worked very hard to teach them to do this. They do not just happen to be sitting still each time. I have heard parents call their children over and over, only to receive a shrug and literal angry little faces. If you do not want this, you must work hard to teach your child to appropriatly respond to your command. Teach them to smile when you call them. You can do this by little games of practice. The correct attitude is expected when eating, when you are giving instruction for dressing, for play, for coming in the house from play, and the list goes on. You'll be so glad when you go to the grocery store, or to church, when you call them and their ears are unplugged. You reap the work you have practiced at home. Some people have remarked many times,"You have story-book children." We know the real story behind the book and smile. It takes hard work and being on guard at all times.

One time when one of our children was around 3 years old and riding a tricycle, her dad said, "Do not go into the road." Lo and behold, he missed her and turned around and she was riding down the country road in front of our house with a little friend trailing behind her. Well, in this instance you can see not only the need to hear the first time, for submission reasons, but also for literal safety reasons. Not listening always leads to dangerous roads . Thankfully, this story has a very good ending… the child was disciplined by dad and from then on there was an indelible etch on her brain to listen. To this day she comes the first time she is called. That spanking was not easy for dad, but the dividends are still paying off today, for that road and many roads of life which could have been detrimental.

Though circumstances and times have changed, there are those who still hold on to traditional values and their big picture and values are in place. In his book, *The Strong Willed Child*, Dr. Dobson explains that spankings should be reserved in response to willful defiance, whenever it occurs (41). Also, it is very important to define early on what is acceptable and unacceptable. The child will have a clear understanding of what you call unacceptable only if you are clear and consistent. Early on, a parent should shake their head and say a firm but loving, "No." If the training begins early on with tappings when the child begins to confront authority, the child will grow accustomed to the response of the consistent disciplining consequence. The consistent nurturing of smiles for affirmation and no's accompanied by consistent tappings will help mold and shape their knowledge of acceptable and unacceptable behavior.

Corporal discipline (consistent taps or pats) applied as early as one year through two years old should work. However, the pain associated with the spanking should be adjusted according to the age/stage or need. A parent cannot allow a child to have his way and then at age 11 and 12 think they will use corporal discipline to get them back in line. Corporal discipline is not a quick fix, e-z pass or drive through McDonalds jiffy fix all. Discipline itself is a process which takes many forms and fashions over the years, and must be applied consistently with love to be effective.

The Hebrew Method - Corporal Discipline

As seen by these two quotes from Proverbs, the Bible clearly supports corporal discipline: "Train up a child in the way he should go: and when he is old, he will not depart from it." (Proverbs 22:6). "He that spareth his rod hateth his son: but he that loveth him chasteneth him betimes" (Proverbs 13:24).

A Step-By-Step Method for Using Corporal Discipline

Who is responsible? The parent who sees the offense needs to take care of the disciplining. If necessary, the discipline should be affirmed by the other mate. I know this can be difficult for a mother, especially, since she is the one usually left at home. My heart does go out to mothers. I remember so many times I could feel resentful, knowing I was usually the one there with the child, resulting in me disciplining them more often than my husband. One thing that helped me, and maybe will help you, is to always remember, "It is better to pay the price for the treasure and enjoy it together than to divide the spoils as enemies." There are some mothers I have known, who kept their kids at bay by constantly saying, "Just wait until your dad comes home, he is going to really punish you." Many times the same mother never told dad and the child learns

Have you ever had a bent wheeled buggy in the grocery store? With no delay you put it back and reach for the next one.

Children can be like bent wheeled buggies, if their will is not broken early.

distrust or the goody, goody mom builds a gap between child and dad, that breaks all future relationships. This kind of home usually ends in a divorce case. The children, by the time they are 14, have learned to trust neither parent. Maybe the dad could have had some effect if he would have been told. Usually this mother has been in abusive situations and has issues that need to be addressed. This kind of mom may have a manipulative subtle spirit (phlegmatic) which is afraid of confrontations and does not know how to overcome fear. This is a very poor way of disciplining. On the other hand, there are dads who offer no assistance because they feel reluctant to come home each day to pull out the correction rod, so to speak. However, a dad really does need to come home with an air of affirmation for mom. This builds trust in the marriage and in the children. If needed, dad should affirm mom's discipline with his own disciplining measure.

Steps of Corporal Discipline
• Privacy: The child should be brought to an area of privacy with the door closed. This is to accomplish a positive behavior, and the purpose will be confused if the child is embarrassed in front of others. When disciplining, there should be no yelling, shouting, or slapping by the parent.
• Affirmation of love should be shown by giving soothing assurance with an arm of love around the shoulders.
• Offense: State the child's offense.
• Authority: Emphasize with the Bible in hand that God's Word places you in care of your child's behavior, and the parent is responsible to God to be obedient.
• Explain your expectations and associate your action with love again. For example, "Johnny, I love you; but because your behavior was unacceptable, I am responsible to God to correct you. Now, if you are not still, if you shout, or withdraw this will call for more correction. Do you understand what I expect?"
• Assess to see if his will is broken. If it has not, there will be no signs of repentance. A broken will is displayed by tears and repentance.
• Affirm your love with a hug of assurance, understanding, and forgiveness.
• Both child and parent should kneel, and then have child to repeat after you a prayer of repentance asking for God's forgiveness.
• Now, it is time to begin all over; a brand new sheet of paper.
• The child needs to wash his face, smile and be ready to meet the family with a cheerful attitude. (He may need a little time for this, depending on age and circumstance.)
• Sometimes it works best to have the child go on up to their room and give them a

space of a set time (10 minutes perhaps) and then they should cheerfully rejoin the family.
• In the meantime, other siblings should be told that they are not to appear as if they notice anything unusual. If there has been an offense to another family member, when the child returns, they are to hug each other and to forgive each other openly.
• Afterwards, the family should be able to go on into life to all that God has for them.

Discipline of this nature will not work unless it is applied constantly and early in a child's life with an equal amount of affection. A child should hear parents tell him everyday, "I love you, Johnny. You mean the world to me." This language of affirmation builds up the child and fills their love tank which Gary Chapman (1995) wrote about in *The Five Love Languages*. This book is very helpful, and I highly recommend it. Also, one should bear in mind that discipline has two sides, like Dr. Dobson says in his book *The Strong Willed Child*. Love has two sides, and both are equally important. The first is constraint with hedges, and the second is assurance with affection. When these two sides of love are administered consistently and steadfastly very early in a child's life, they will yield pleasant fruit for both parent and child.

The Report Writing Method
There are other means of disciplining that work well, especially after ages 12 and 13. If your child continues to have a generally poor attitude, it may be good to have them write a series of reports, once a week for five weeks. The number will vary according to the severity of the offense. For instance, if you are teaching responsibility and the child continually fails in making his bed, and you have tried the charts and all the positive rewards to no avail, and now you are out of ideas, you may suggest that Johnny write a report for you about the responsibilities that he has in the family. Give him guidelines, such as defining the word from a dictionary. The report should be at least three paragraphs long with examples of what happens when someone fails to fulfill their responsibilities. Other subjects can include self-discipline, setting the alarm clock, showing respect to elders, showing respect to family members, etc. Be sure to set a time limit for when this report is due.

Order in the Home
Webster's defines order as an authoritative direction or instructive command, a condition in which each thing is properly disposed with reference to other things and to its purpose methodically, or harmonious arrangement. A couple should apply this definition to their way of thinking before marriage so that when they are married they

Relationships
have more
power than any
discipline
technique.
Cynthia Tobias

will have order and harmony in their home. One esteemed friend of mine brought a picture of order to her home by using star constellations. I especially liked this since it has to do with this book's theme of stars. One should consider the balance of purpose and relationships to the other. In this particular comparison, each planet has an orbit, and the sun and moon have their positions. The home where dad shines like the sun and mom, like the moon, reflects his leadership and brings life to the children who, like the planets, revolve in their appointed places. Everyone working together in their own sphere will bring joy and peace to the relationship. Just as a fraction of an inch off may bring collision to planets if they were to spin off of their normal rotation patterns, likewise the chaos caused from members of a household not staying within their position cannot be overemphasized.

Proper authority in contrast to parental power is defined as loving leadership. Without decision-makers and others who agree to follow, there is inevitable chaos and confusion and disorder in human relationships. Loving authority is the glue that holds social orders together, and it is absolutely necessary for the healthy functioning of a family.

> My son, hear the instruction of thy father, and forsake not the law of thy mother:
> for they shall be an ornament of grace unto thy head and chains about thy neck.
> Proverbs 1:8-9

The String - The Guiding Line

The string of the kite is used to illustrate the guideline discipline provides. While the string is definitely the love attachment as we saw in chapter 1, this string also gives guidance. The same string that attaches is used to discipline in this chapter. Dr. James Dobson's book, *Tough Love*, offers the same philosophy. There are two sides to love. While you stand with your attachments of love and affirmation in place, the same love has to be tough in order to serve as a guiding force. Just as the kite needs string to help it catch the up-draft to fly, it also needs a taunt string to keep it in the air. If we give the kite too much slack, it will tumble out of the sky. The challenge for parents, then, in disciplining their child is learning how to keep a balance between affectionate love and tough love, giving them the emotional attachment while maintaining firm boundaries or guidelines.

In our study of discipline, we have covered the restraints used to keep our children "headed in the right direction." Next in our study, we will consider the motivational elements which "turn their motor on because they want to."

The Motivational Factors

Sears put into words the fact that children who taste winning in one area are set up to become winners in others. Taking this into consideration, the logical thing to do is to find the one area that your child can shine early on. The Shine Technique uses talent and recreation as the motivational end pieces to sandwich in the character and academics parents need to teach.

Build a Shine Sandwich

- 1st layer…. Turn motor of child on with a talent or recreation incentive (motivation) key
- 2nd layer… Work on academics, character, talent
- 3rd layer… Offer talent or recreation incentive key for motivation to keep child moving towards next door of his age level life
- His interest in talent/ and recreation/life? (child's profile) first slice of Bread
- (Example Child) Reaching for age level 9 while still only age 8
- At 8 years of age, parent says… "Okay, you want to learn to play the trumpet?"
- Make an appointment to go check out an instrument, starting with rent to buy. The goal of owning his very own instrument should be used as leverage to inspire practice and effort.
- Teach him the responsibilities of self-discipline, practice schedules, and self-control (Meat)
- Consequences restrain (Recreation your child enjoys) (Last piece of bread)

The key to motivation is finding a talent and recreation your child enjoys.

The Shine Technique for Discipline Uses This Underlying Principle

This is a smart technique with a built-in disciplining program. It uses the child's natural talents and hobbies as the motivational leverage to keep them moving in the right direction of character and academics. Since your objective is to help the child become, you are on a forward move. Your parenting homework is to think ahead of what you want your child to become. The objective is to offer incentives to keep everything moving forward. The best incentives are the real life ones like what's coming next. At ages 4, 5, 6, incentives might be Friday at McDonald's; or at 7, 8, 9, learning to play a musical instrument may be next. At ages 10, 11, 12, incentives may be youth group night. At ages 13, 14, 15, incentives could be the preparation years that culminate in earning a driver's license and keys to the car. At ages 16, 17, 18, incentives could move to youth trips and conferences. The opposite side of this is, if the parent does not keep things moving forward with positive incentives, then the child may keep moving toward the negative. For example, the child threatens if you don't do so and so, I am going to get that or I'm going to do this.

After you look at this motivational process, you may think, there is nothing new about this process. Please, continue reading. You are correct; the plan is simple, and the positive award system has been used many times. However, the tricky part for the parent is finding the motivation that keeps their child going through the right doors at each age. This is the part that you will find useful in the "Shine" parenting technique. If enacted correctly, this program offers a built-in study guide to "find your child" – to maximize his unique gifts and motivate him at each stage of life.

(Also explained in chapter 3)

The Process of building a "Shine" Parenting Disciplining Program is as stated below:

1. Build a Child's Shine Profile (you can start this as early as 1 yr. old but you add to it yearly or as needed)
2. Decide a talent (try a few)
3. Character skill to be taught (age appropriate)
4. Academic skills needed (age appropriate)
5. Social preparation for next growth level
6. Use the above information as your motivational leverage for keeping him moving in the direction you are guiding
7. Use your best parenting style for offering the restraining guide (this is discussed in the section after building the Shine Profile)
8. Celebrate your child's achievement in a positive direction - The Shine

Star Parenting

Child's Shine Profile: Real Life Responsibilities vs. Real Life Incentives

In the following sample sheet, notice that each responsibility, character, skill, and talent is motivated by a real-life incentive that is not monetarily oriented. (A blank sheet is provided in the appendix.)

Sample Information Sheet for Building Shine Profile

Age	Responsibility	Talent	Character	Incentive
2-3	Hygiene or skill	Music, art, craft	Obedience	Daily. Small treats or stickers
4-5	Hygiene or skill Trash, Make bed	Practice Letters	Sharing	Big Friday McDonalds
6-8	Trash, make bed, clean sink, vacuum (8)	Practice Reading	Manners	A class they enjoy, sports, gym
9-11	Trash, mow yard, make bed and clean room	Practices on Rental INSTRUMENT looking forward to own	Self Control	New instrument Trumpet… etc
12-15	Awake with alarm clock. Do all the above Clean closet & help with kitchen chores	Own instrument, practice, recitals	Respect	Involve with extra curricular conferences, etc. Driver's license
16-18	All the Above Keep car washed	Continues practice, recitals	9 Characteristics listed in Chapter 5	Drive car College choices

Good parents keep their hand on the string and fly the kite. The kite cannot fly itself or it will never get off the ground or stay in the sky. So off to High Hope's Hill we go… Happy Flying!

My Child's Shine Profile

Name: _____

Age: _____

Basic Personality Type: _____

Best Learning Style: _____

What you want them to excel in?

Academically _____

Character _____

Talent _____

In sports he/she likes _____

In music he/she would like to play _____

He/She likes to hum and sing with the music _____

He/She likes to speak _____

He/she loves poetry and likes to read _____

He/She enjoys crafts _____

Train and move forward by using the Door of Life Incentive Shine Plan, blending natural life incentives (personal style) with consequences.

Parenting Styles

We have studied different motivational styles needed in disciplining; now we want to think of the restraining measures needed.

The Four Parenting Styles

Which parenting style will work best for this situation and this child? The point is that we all can be one or the other at different times in our lives. For example, when under stress, you may be more totalitarian or shooting star in your style. When you are frustrated by your child's immaturity or irresponsibility and decide to handle everything yourself, you may become manipulative or fiber optic in your style. Few of us fall completely into one category or the other. Thus, it is important that parents assess the consequences of the various parenting styles. One may be said to be too laid back, permissive, or just plain neglectful. The other may be too overbearing, authoritative, or abusive. As you study the consequences of the following parenting styles, keep in mind that parents must be responsible for the choices they make and their actions as parents.

Shooting Star – Totalitarian Parenting

The shooting star style of parenting usually goes along with a sanguine or choleric temperament. Sanguine personalities are impulsive, nice, fun people; however, when they get pushed down long enough, they will impulsively blow their stack. For instance, they have tolerated a whiney toddler for forty days plus now, and the whiney toddler knocks over mommy's fine china doll. Impulsively, the nice, sanguine mommy goes into a rage – hollering, shouting, threatening, slapping, or all of the above. On the other hand, the choleric personality, while not thought to be so nice, would be giving his drill sergeant commands all along to the whiney toddler. According to scientists, stars must ignite with the atmospheric derivatives around them to keep burning. When this no longer happens, they begin burning inwardly causing a burnout, hence creating falling stars or shooting stars.

Shooting star parents command: Give me those keys! You are grounded for 40 days! Shut up! (Shout, slap the face, or push and shove, etc.) They go off the deep end and make harsh, unreasonable threats, and basically lose control. The message they send to their children through their harsh scolding is, "You are a bother." Shooting star parents are capable of resorting to abusive language and becoming physically violent.

People, like stars, keep their shine brightest by always burning outwardly. But when both begin to burn inwardly, they become falling stars.

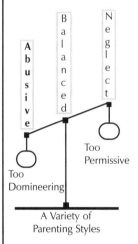

A Variety of
Parenting Styles

113

Their children may think they have failed forever or their parents do not love or respect them.

If your personality and parenting style leans toward that of the shooting star, the following confrontational skills can help you change the way you deal with your children when they frustrate you.

Confrontational Skills
"Cool Handles for Hot Pots"
The "I" message vs. the "You" message
Talk so kids will listen and listen to kids when they talk.

Praise and Self Esteem
Instead of evaluating, describe!
Describe What You See.
Example: I see a clean carpet, a smooth bed, and toys neatly lined up.
Describe How this Makes You Feel.
Example: I really like walking into this bedroom. It makes me feel happy!
Focus on Behavior
Example: I need help picking these things up now.
Explain Why Bad Behavior is Not Acceptable.
Example: I do not like it when I see mud on the floor.
Invites Cooperation
Example: I cannot hear you when you scream.

Focus on Child
Example: You sure made a mess.
Blames the Child
Example: You ought to be ashamed.
Invites Uncooperativeness
Example: You better shut up!
(Handout in Appendix)

Wandering Star – Permissive Parenting
Wandering Star Passive... I wonder where that star is?
Messages sent:
- I have my life, my job, and my education. I hope your's turns out okay.
- You are a bother.
- You will not keep me from my life.
- Your problems are the result of someone else's.
- I do not need to be home with you.

Message sent:
- TV? Watch what you want.
- Do what you want, as long as you don't bother me.

Fiber Optic Star Plug In – Manipulative Parenting

Fiber optic star parents are the automatic plugs that assume all responsibilities for the child, including the child's responsibilities; and if their plug does not work, then they manipulate or blame others.
The messages they send:

- · You are fragile
- · You are always right
- · You need me to make your world work
- · You are non-functional without me
- · You are non-functional, and it is everyone else's fault.

The Big Dipper Style – Balanced Parenting

The Big Dipper Style of parenting represents the constellation by the name which is easily spotted. The Big Dipper is constant in its position and forms the shape of a kite and or big dipper. For our lesson's sake, the Big Dipper represents the balanced, negotiable parenting style. It offers love in her cup and guidance from her constant light. It offers respect instead of embarrassment and trust because of consistency

The Best Star

Shooting Star , Wandering Star, and Fiber Optic Plug-in

Negative consequences of these three parenting styles:

- • Abusive
- • Neglectful
- • Non-functional

Unfortunately, the negative consequences inherent in those particular parenting styles lead to the following problems:

- • Teenage rebellion
- • Distrust for authority
- • Disrespect for authority

The best style takes time to explain... and offers choices and time limits.

Big Dipper Stars Form Balanced Discipline

Teach consequences for behavior

- • Seeks to encourage self-esteem but not encourage wrong behavior. Example: I love you, but I do not like what you did.
- • Loves the child but points out unacceptable behavior
- • Seeks to have correct consequence, not power struggle
- • Seeks to lift up, not embarrass
- • Seeks to teach, not to hurt
- • Seeks to show respect for child and parent

115

Design Star Consequential Situations for Behavior:
Use reflective Communication Style.

Cleaning Bedroom _____;

Doing Chores _____.

Example: I noticed clothes on the bed. I need you to hang up the clothes on the bed; because when you don't, I feel you don't care about your bedroom. You may choose to either hang up your clothes before we eat dinner or do it afterwards instead of going over to your friend's house.

Kite Talk:
Evaluation for Chapter 4
Circle the correct answer which best illustrates effective, respectful disciplining.

Cleaning Bedroom & Doing Chores

I noticed clothes on your bed.
A.   Clean up your room you lazy bum.
B.   I need you to hang up your clothes. When you don't, I feel you do not appreciate your belongings.
C.   I need you to hang up your clothes before dinner, because when you don't I feel you do not appreciate your belongings. If you choose to wait, you can do it after dinner instead of visiting your friend.

(Scene is at church in front of peers)
John is 10 years old. Mom sees him talking to a group of boys she has told him not to. She should:
A.   Go to him with glaring eyes, swat him on the arm, and say, "Get over here like I told you."
B.   Holler from where she is, "Johnny, get over here. Haven't I told you never to hang around these guys?"
C.   Quietly go to circle of peers and speak kind words to them and with unnoticeable eye contact, say softly, "John, I have an important message I need to give you. Thank you for coming with me; you can rejoin your friends soon."

·   Name the four basic parenting styles.

_____

·   Do you remember the four disciplining techniques?

_____

Which discipline method would you use for each case below:
·   Johnny spilled the milk and started crying.

_____

·   Annie is always late coming to breakfast before school. You have threatened to leave her, but today she has already made you 5 minutes late. What will you do?

_____

·   You have warned 10 year old Sam that his room is not to be left undone. What will you do? He has left his bed unmade, his shoes out in the middle of the floor, and several articles of clothing left on the floor where he was dressing. What will you do?

_____

·   Lately 12 year old George has been testing everything you say. He becomes critical, argumentive, and always has a comeback even when he is told to be quiet. What do you do?

_____

·   A mother asks her son in a polite way to empty the trash. Son belligerently throws his head around and glaringly looks at mother and says, "I am not going to empty the trash can."

_____

·   Watch for subtle open defiance. Mother ask son in a polite way to empty trash. Son quietly walks out of the house without doing what his mother asked.

_____

STAR DUST

PRINCE AND PRINCESS IN TRAINING

ETIQUETTE, DATING, AND HARD-TO-DISCUSS ISSUES

STAR DUST
PRINCE AND PRINCESS
IN TRAINING
ETIQUETTE, DATING, AND
HARD-TO-DISCUSS ISSUES

Leadership Character

The clock struck 12:00, and she ran away leaving a trail of wonder. Where did the princess go? Prince Royal was sure to find her. All of us know our little ones have it in them, if we could just find that magic wand. Take heart, while no one is really perfect, with a lot of hard work, we can have the princess and prince reign supreme. Developing the prince and the princess within requires developing the social graces that keep the annoyances down and build up the graceful side. It is putting on a Christ-like spirit and taking off anything that doesn't become Him.

The Fountain of Everlasting Beauty

The word of God declares, "… we have this treasure in earthen vessels, that the excellency of the power may be of God, and not of us" (II Corinthians 4:7). This treasure that Paul refers to is God's Holy Spirit. Beauty that glorifies God's treasure, which is inside of us, is the only true beauty. Anything that promotes self or brings glory to our flesh will in time fade. Isn't it good to know there is hope for beauty that does last? God intends for His people to shine forth His light: "Ye are the light of the world. A city that is set on an hill cannot be hid" (Matthew 5:14). God intends for His children to bring Him glory.

Again as is written in God's Word, His people are a royal priest-hood: "But ye are a chosen generation, a royal priesthood, an holy nation, a peculiar people; that ye should shew forth the praises of him who hath called you out of darkness into his marvelous light…" (I Peter 2:9). The Bible also states that the Lord has made us both kings and priests (Revelation 1:6; 5:10). From this royal lineage shall come princes and princesses. Becoming a prince or princess in the way we walk, sit, and stand exemplifies Christian character.

Star Talk ☆

Public Manners

Mothers and fathers who start teaching habits that are pleasing for public ethics to their children at a young age enjoy the "Shine."

Kite Talk:

Watch out! Don't get hung up on these Hang-ups!
Recommended Reading: George Washington's *Civility Ethics*

When George Washington was a youth, he was required to write and learn civility ethics. These rules originated in France and were circulated to other countries. Dating from 1745, the notebook in George Washington's own hand was written during the time he was attending school in Fredericksburg, Virginia. It contains some 110 "Rules of Civility in Conversation Amongst Men." It appears some of these simple ethics have been pushed by the wayside. I highly recommend reading his civility ethics and have included below twelve rules from George Washington that bear practice in our modern age.

Twelve Stars of Public Behavior:

1. Every action in company ought to be with some sign of respect to those present.
2. It is good manners to prefer them to whom we speak before ourselves, especially if they be above us with whom in no sort we ought to begin.
3. Let your discourse with men of business be short and comprehensive.
4. Strive not with your superiors in argument, but always submit your judgment to others with modesty. Undertake not to teach your equal in the art he himself professes, it savors of arrogancy.
5. Being to advise or reprehend anyone, consider, whether it ought to be in public or in private, presently or at some other time, also in what terms to do it, and in reproving show no signs of choler, but do it with sweetness and mildness.
6. Wherein you reprove another be unblamable yourself, for example is more prevalent than precept.
7. Be not forward, but friendly and courteous, the first to salute, hear and answer, and be not pensive when it is time to converse.
8. Go not thither where you know not whether you shall be welcome or not. Force not advice without being asked, and when desired, do it briefly.
9. If two contend together, take not the part of either, unconstrained, and be not obstinate in your opinion, in things indifferent be of the major side.
10. Reprehend not the imperfection of others, for that belongs to parents and masters.
11. Be not angry at the table, whatever happens: and if you have reason to be so show it not: put on a cheerful countenance, especially if there be strangers, for good humor makes one dish a feast.
12. Labor to keep alive in your breast that little spark of celestial fire called conscience.

Prince and Princess in Training

Social Graces

Children and youth should be taught to cover their mouth with a Kleenex to sneeze and cough. (Most burping is not a spontaneous reaction and, with exerting self-control, can be altered. Tums and Maalox can help with upset stomach and keep you from being embarrassed by obnoxious odors. There are other products on the market that are effective, also.) It is nice to smile and even chuckle at the table, but if it brings a deep guffawing laugh, it is unbecoming to open your mouth widely. This can bring an unbecoming exposure of your teeth and mouth cavity.

As young children sit and eat, parents need to always pray over their food. Soon they will be repeating the prayers for themselves. Children as young as 2-3 need to learn to keep their food and hands to themselves. Parents can help these social graces by practicing them consistently at home. (Keeping their mouth closed and not talking with food in their mouths is taught by consistent and loving parents).

Please help your child be aware of unpleasant breath and habitual annoyances. Many times because of sinus drainage, the gum tissue of the mouth and tongue becomes a reservoir for unpleasant odors. Brushing often and using breath mints and chewing gum can help. Nagging sniffles on a date can be an unpleasant annoyance but can be eliminated with proper care and allergy medication.

There is nothing more refreshing on a date than to feel free to smile. Cleanliness of your teeth makes your smile brighter and gives you a fresh demeanor. Brush your teeth often using a good toothbrush. Use whitening toothpaste, whitening strips, or other whitening products often. Cleanliness of ears can be double-checked with swabs. Talking with food in your mouth is obnoxious to the listeners and lessens your chance for a good friendship. It shows you are inconsiderate of others.

Before you begin to speak at the table, wait until you are finished with your food, cover your mouth with the end of your napkin, gently wipe your mouth area, and then begin your conversation.

The art of good communication while eating or any time involves listening as well as speaking. It is a skill where the word compliance should be practiced regularly. Yielding to the one who spoke first shows respect for the other person and also reflects well of the person listening. It is like someone is saying, "What you have to say is very important to me." Have you ever been around anyone that you really respected and were excited

Parents can help social graces by practicing them consistently at home.

because you were going to eat dinner with your hero? Then, as the dinner progressed, they talked, and talked, and talked… never giving you the opportunity to share a word. In fact, they acted as if they didn't care to hear you. Some friendships never bud because of a thoughtless person who never gave the other person a chance to speak but held a one-sided conversation.

Good Grooming

Pay attention to the details. While we may not be millionaires, we can dress well. We can make sure our clothes are pressed and appropriately chosen for the occasion. Our shoes, accessories, and hair always need to be neat. There are numerous hair-styles, and just because a new fad comes along doesn't mean that we need to try it if it doesn't become us. On the other hand, it is refreshing to have new styles. Everyone appreciates the effort that someone spends trying to help their appearance.

(A Word for the Princess) In the olden days, the princess would gird herself and have layers and layers under their outer garment. While we may not need as many layers, clothing should lay smooth and be in good taste. A full length mirror for front and back would help to make sure undergarments do not show. This is the mark of a true princess. (The unkempt pony-tail with a sloppy sweat shirt and jean skirt is not what we want others to think of Christ.) We need to be comfortable and dressed for the occasion, but in a manner of Christ-like spirit. Know ye not whose temple ye are. We have the power to glorify Him, and we have the power to shame Him.

Inner Beauty

Young ladies should be taught the young lady who is virtuous will not become immodest in dress, speech, or action. The Bible teaches that a young lady's meek and quiet spirit is the beauty that is to be desired (I Peter 3:1-6). An example of godliness is modesty of speech and projection of the voice when with a group. Choose words which are examples of Godly character and speech which reflects Godliness. Girls will want to be light–hearted so they are not thought to be a dead pan, but not so frivolous that everything they say sounds ecstatic or appears insincere. For a girl to lean on a guy around others is not respectful or Godly. Displays of affection should be done alone and that with the parent's permission in their home.

Another example of social propriety is when entering a room where a group of people you know are, wave and speak hello loud enough for everyone to hear you, then with a graceful smile, start talking in lower tones to someone near-by. If in a crowd, gracefully make your way through the group, mingling and being friendly to all. Sometimes it is easier or more comfortable to get with one particular person and stay with them the entire evening, but it is only courteous and considerate to make yourself friendly to all, especially if you are the host or the hostess.

The atmosphere when you eat can be queenly or your behavior can model the unfortunate ill-bred. There are three things to remember if you want to digest your food in good order and pleasantly.

What you have to say is very important to me.

The Art of Pleasant Communication:
1. Communication: (listening as well as speaking), observing polite eating habits and being well-mannered.
2. Compliance: acting in accordance of a request, demand, order rule, etc, and to be formally polite.
3. Star Dust: "Yield at the table for others to speak." Practice games at the table giving each other the turn to speak." My daughter Cherie places a box of cards with pictures on the table… (it came from McDonald's), and each family member pulls a card and makes up a description at the dinner table and the others have to guess what it is. (The game is much like Pictionary). This game makes eating more fun for small children and enhances conversation for more mature ones.

If you are the host, you are responsible for setting a nice table with candles glowing and soft background music. (Make the environment suitable to the occasion).

Star Dust
Correct posture looks wholesome, happy, and shows an eager attitude of a submissive spirit. Scripture teaches that a submissive spirit is "an ornament of grace unto thy head, and chains about thy neck" (Proverbs 1:9).

1. Wise children listen to the instruction of their Godly mother and father. (Proverbs 1:8)
2. A submissive spirit beautifies the countenance.
3. When approaching an elder, one should step aside as to allow them to pass first. This shows respect.
4. When speaking to one another, one should hold your head up and pleasantly look into the eyes as this shows respect.

Kite Talk:
Closet Care: A good place to get hung up!
The way you take care of your clothes speaks of what kind of person you are. If you wear wrinkled clothes, are you being considerate of others? When you dress your best, you are showing respect to others by saying, "Your friendship means the world to me, and I am showing you this by dressing my very best." A place for everything in your closet may take time, but when you are dressing, you will be so glad you can find what you need. Look for tie racks, scarf racks, shoe and accessory racks. Properly hung clothes pay huge dividends. For one thing, think of the time saved not having to iron!

Star Talk ☆

For the Prince
A true prince always opens the door for his princess and also treats her like a princess in all situations by assessing her needs before meeting his.

Dating Preparation
For your kite to not fall out of the sky during these turbulent times calls for advance preparation. How well you are prepared will determine your kite's ability to endure during these tough and yet thrilling flights. Somewhere, between the age of puberty and 18, a natural phenomenon for young people occurs – they want to date. As parents we all want our children to have natural attractions and desires; however, the main thing is maintaining family harmony while allowing our young kites the opportunity to fly without wrecking.

Questions that you and your children may ask in preparation for dating may sound like the following:
- What is the appropriate age for dating?
- When is a first kiss okay?
- Where are the safety zones in affection?
- Are there any limits to safe dating, and if so, what are they?
- What is maturity level?
- What behaviors are indicators of maturity level?
- How do I present guidelines as a parent to my children and their friends so they will be responsive and respected?

To exemplify Christ in our bodies, we should strive toward mastery of one's carriage.

Preparation for this time is truly a process. The ideal situation is for you to prepare your child for this time of their life by first of all developing a trusting relationship, consistent prayer life, and open heart-to-heart talks.

126

One suggestion our family has tried and thought worked well was having a special night set aside for an individual child with dad or mom night. A night out with dad or mom at a nice restaurant where the atmosphere is relaxed and dad lays out a plan for the on-coming years has worked for us. Candlelight and a loving parent giving guidelines from the heart makes cherished and unforgettable memories.

Shine
 By using age and the 'Shine' technique with the doors of life incentives, you can offer love and leverage. Another idea is to give them journals with your love letter in the front alluding to responsibility but written in love. For instance, for our daughter, Angela Faith's 15th birthday, we gave her a journal, in which I wrote the following about her name:

Happy Birthday Angela,

 Angela, I am so proud of you. I will never forget when you were born, a beautiful, brown-haired doll. You lay on the table so compliant and confident. True to my first impression, that is what you have always been. You have shown dad and I what your name really meant, for you have really been our Angel and anchor of faith through many storms. Your consistent nature has been just like your middle name, Faith. We thought you would be a boy, but God lovingly knew what we really needed for the time and gave us an Angel of Faith. We needed you before we needed anything else, for unless we were anchored in faith, we were never going to be complete. That is what our lives would be like without you, our Angel of Faith, incomplete. You have lived up to your name whole heartedly. Your dad and I are so proud of you. We know on your 15th birthday we have given our children the privilege of group dating. May you continue to give us reasons to believe in you. One day you will be 16 and you will want to drive, then you will look forward to the day you will want to date alone. Angela, how you handle your freedom now will determine the freedom you gain for yourself later. Your attitude of love and obedience around us in small matters will determine how well we think you can make judgment calls when car keys and boyfriends and other places start calling. When you walk down the aisle, may the color white of your dress truly reflect your character as it does now. We are privileged to be your parents. We love you, our Angel. Keep flying High... our Angel of Faith...
 All my love,
 Mother

Dating Age

Making the decision for the age of maturity is a vital decision all parents should consider and pray intensely concerning the best time for their children. After much prayer and reading, we decided we would follow the advice given from Beverly Lahaye's book entitled, *Understand Your Child's Temperment* (1997). As recommended, we set the age of 15 for our children to group date. This means going with other young people in a car and calling a particular person their date. However, it could not be a couple thing until age 16, and no dating alone until age 18. This plan prevents many unnecessary worries and situations alone.

Affection and exploiting the body is nothing more than sensual desires. The effects of premarital sex are heartrending, and yet the statistics are growing. Out-of-wedlock births seem to be a cycle that renders its pain over and over again; and its tidal-wave effects rock the foundation of rich and poor alike, not giving preference for race or status in life. Statistics show that premarital sex and out-of-wedlock births is a reoccurring cycle in individuals – once they begin this habit, it is difficult to end. However, statistics taken from the same group show that those going to church have a higher rate of abstinence. Counseling and support groups in churches offer much to the needy and disadvantaged, and help them break the cycle. (Statistics may be found in chapter 1, pg. 13)

Dating Readiness

In this manual, our efforts are geared toward helping parents rationalize which parenting skills bring the best results. We advocate high levels of consequential rationalizing in order to make proper decisions concerning maturity levels of readiness. If a parent has followed through on disciplining with consequential maturity through the years and not just for dating readiness, then the results are even higher levels of readiness and better outcomes. Here again if a high level of consequential rationalizing has not been properly nurtured, maintained, and proven, then a child's impulsive desires will win.

We give firm advice that you should teach a young man to respect a young lady. (This seems to be unnecessary to address; however, statistics prove we must address this obvious issue.) We teach our daughters that it would be best if they would not allow a young man to kiss them until they really know him and have their parents permission. During this time, a wise youth will not proceed with a relationship at all unless their parents are in true approval. They need to develop a friendship, and if the young man has a star character reflecting that of a Godly man, then a relationship will develop in a friendship manner. We believe a young person should be 18 years old at least to be able to make this decision.

We try to place it in the hearts of our children that their name is the only thing they really have and once they loose it, it cannot be bought back. That is why your family attending a church where the pastor and youth group take a strong stand for righteous living will give support and strength concerning matters which you are advocating. Youth, who come under the authority of parents and church guidelines, will be the winners. They will not have to suffer the hardships brought on by promiscuous lifestyles. Let me insert here that if one should make a mistake, let us remember the forgiving story of the rose. Let us not continue to justify sin, but by the same token, we must love, forgive, and go on with our lives, for this is God's way, the best way.

Hard to Talk About Issues

What about friends with different values? Most of the time if parents are around their children's friends on a regular basis, they will know what is going on (although even following this standard does not eliminate surprises at times). To avoid your child being alone with friends that they may not know well, the first rule of thumb is to invite them to your home. If this is not convenient, go to a restaurant together. As a parent, it is your responsibility to get to know your child's peers. I asked one mother who has two grown, reputable sons what her guideline was, and she said she never allowed her son to sleep over at anyone's house, other than cousins, until he was twelve. She felt by then he could take care of himself if he was placed in the wrong kind of situation. Why do some parents feel they should have rules but at graduation parties and other special parties the rules don't apply? Children should know you have a set of guidelines… and one of those rules should be that you can appear at any moment. They should know if anyone at a friend's house is violating the principles you as parents have set that they should dismiss themselves and come home. We are talking about purity and keeping our children from drugs and alcohol. Allowing your child the privilege of riding in a vehicle with another young person should be a great honor and one of the doors of responsibility.

How do you get a handle on important topics that need discussion such as puberty, premarital sex, internet guidelines, drug and alcohol awareness, and intervention issues? When children are around nine, ten, at least by age twelve, according to your own judgment, they will need to be given direction as to what is going on in their bodies. For young men, a night out with dad, perhaps a camping trip makes a perfect memory. Dad could bring a book (Dr. James Dobson's *Bringing Up Boys*, for example). Dr. Dobson also has tapes of this book that father and son can listen to together if they would like. The main thing is to let boys know they are normal and that everything that is going on in their bodies is natural. This important time between father and son becomes a bonding time. If you have a son, I strongly recommend reading *Bringing Up Boys*.

Mother and daughter spending a night away brings a special time together for heart talks. One mother shared this as being one of the highlights in her and her daughter's life. Having a clinical book on hand might be of some help. Special tapes to listen to together help a daughter feel special, creating loving memories and straight to the heart talks. This would also be a good time to talk to them about sensitive subjects such as homosexual issues, AIDS and venereal diseases, drug and alcohol abuse, etc. You may also access Drug and Alcohol Awareness programs in your community.

Titus 2:11-12 teaches us to live a life of self-control, not fulfilling our passions but living self controlled, upright and godly lives: "For the grace of God that bringeth salvation hath appeared to all men, teaching us that, denying ungodliness and worldly lusts, we should live soberly, righteously, and godly, in this present world."

Young boys and young girls need to be taught life lessons about pro-life and promiscuity. One church leader takes their young girls to a women's shelter when they teach the young ladies about teen pregnancy. They also take their young boys to visit a home for teen violence.

Kite Talk:
Evaluation For Chapter 5

Recall two correct ideas for each number.
Section I.
1.   Posture while sitting or standing and getting into and out of a car

_____

2.   Good manners while eating

_____

3.   Prayer at table

_____

4.   Grooming

_____

5.   Proper care of teeth and oral hygiene

_____

6.   Conversation at the table

_____

7.   Clothing and closet care

_____

Below are a review of questions that you and your children may ask in preparation for dating. You may not only save your child but your home by being prepared to answer these questions in mutual agreement with your mate using a proven source as your guide. The most proven is the guide found in the Word of God.

Section II.
What is the appropriate age for dating?
      · When is a first kiss okay?
      · Where are the safety zones in affection?
      · Are there any limits to safe dating, and if so, what are they?
      · What is maturity level?
      · What behaviors are indicators of maturity level?
      · How do I present guidelines as a parent to my children and their friends so they will be
        responsive and respected?

Section III.
Give an example of how you can talk to your son or daughter about "hard-to-talk about issues."

_____

KITE FLYING TIPS

ENDURANCE (STRESS AND ANGER MANAGEMENT)
LIFESTYLES AND ENVISIONING STARS

CHAPTER 6

KITE FLYING TIPS

ENDURANCE (STRESS AND ANGER MANAGEMENT)
LIFESTYLES AND ENVISIONING STARS

Stress Management for Parent and Child

My husband and I were passing a church when one of us noticed a very humorous and catchy marquis, "Moses was a basket case, too!" "There is hope," I thought. In the New Testament, Paul was also a basket case. Thankfully, they were rescued and divinely brought to safety.

On September 24, 2001, President George W. Bush spoke these words in a proclamation to the families of America: "Strong families make a strong America." When it comes to our homeland being under attack, nothing is more under attack than our own homes. In America today, we find the roles we play as parents can be very stressful. The times we live in are very stressful because of events such as 9/11/2001, the Christmas tsunami of 2004, and also the hurricanes that devastated the city of New Orleans and the Gulf Coast in 2005, where thousands of lives were gone in a matter of minutes. The uncertainty of our future can cause an underlying unrest. Yet the most frightening of all uncertainties is not those across the ocean, but the fading picture of homes giving way to violence and fragmented relationships. It is time for us all to ask where the lifelines are that we can use to pull our family safely to shore.

Safety Ropes - Identifying Stress Signals
Be aware of these symptoms so you can identify stress in your child. The following are tell-tale indicators of childhood stress:
- Irritability
- Whiney
- Violence, especially in small children
- Suddenly can't do things for themselves
- Doesn't want to sleep by themselves
- Can't get along with others in school or play

Areas that cause stress for children and teens are:
- Changing routines
- Illness
- Changing locations
- Recent divorce
- New baby
- Unstable home life
- Inconsistent
- Never knowing who will be home

Adult consequences for not managing stress
Burn-out Syndrome:
- Depression
- Not interested in life
- Physical and mental break downs
- Mood shifts
- Anger becomes unmanageable
- Violence or passive behavior that affects others
- Irritability
- Finally, a general inability to function because of inability to make sound judgments

Who is Responsible?

In essence, it is the parent's job to make healthy choices concerning their own stress management and the management of their children. Below are some ideas for thought:

Physical

When a person engages in physical exercise, the mind is especially affected. During physical exercise, the body releases hormones into the mind that actually help a person think more clearly. Exercise also increases blood flow and elevates the oxygen level creating a temporary rush improving the body's energy level. The following is a list of suggested physical activities:
- Enjoy walking in a park, running, yard work (if this is a release), any physical activity that is enjoyed.
- Physical exercise is one of the best ways to relieve daily tension because it involves the well-being of the whole body: heart, respiratory and vascular systems, and the muscles. Physical exercise

is an especially good way to relieve anger and tension.

Mental

The mind is closely associated with the body and spirit; and when a person is stressed, it becomes very hard for them to distinguish between mental, physical, or spiritual stress. However, if you have a job that requires mentally taxing work or if you have to deal with a lot of issues, such as counseling, you probably need daily mental release. The following are ways to relieve mental stress:

- Enjoy bath and aroma therapy, including saunas and/or swimming.
- Drink soothing tea, such as herbal hot tea like chamomile, mint, or peach.
- Experience music therapy: soothing music brings rest to a tired mind and soul. David played the harp to sooth Saul's irritated mind.
- Participate in activities: change your activities; get away from routine; take a trip if possible.
- Have dinner with a favorite person.
- Participate in art and other hobbies like gourmet cooking, etc.

Spiritual

A person's spirit affects both a person's physical and mental health; therefore, daily attention to the spirit is of vital importance. Regular church attendance and Christian fellowship help keep the human spirit strong, but daily prayer, meditation, and Bible reading are the best resources for a renewed spirit.

- Spiritual... Redefine your faith in God.
- Practice daily meditation and devotion.
- Spiritual strength is the true essence to life.

Helping Children Release their Tension

- Involve their schedule with physical exercise daily.
- Family meals should be a time of reconnecting and reaffirming.
- Make a special time to be alone with the child.
- Read a special book together (even teens like this)
- Try to talk about the not so important so that talking about the important will come easier.
- After a move, see that your schedule gets into a routine for the child as soon as possible.

Dearest Mom, ...It would take more than one book to truly write all the wonderful memories of my childhood, the ups and the downs and of course, all those late night cups of coffee, Mom.

With all my Love, Your Baby girl, Cherie'

Anger Management

Webster defines anger as a strong feeling of displeasure aroused by a wrong or a supposed wrong. Its function serves as a defensive mechanism that energizes the body when given certain signals. It is used to express strong feelings and disrupts thinking ability. Unbridled anger produces inappropriate behavioral displays such as rage, yelling, and often violence such as slapping, hitting, or physically hurting someone in some fashion.

Maintaining Control When You or Your Child are Inappropriately Angry

Signals - Learn to watch for signals in your child that show he is becoming upset. In yourself, learn to alert yourself when there is a strong feeling about certain issues. Lower your voice immediately after the first "cue" of a possible situation coming your way. Think of it as a tornado. If it hits, it has the ability to destroy everything you have built.

Time Out - At the first tinge that your child is headed for the rocks, bring him to a safe cove. By isolating him in time-out, you are removing him from the location where he is stirred up in an unsafe zone. Changing scenes sometimes causes one to think clearer. Let them sit quietly for a while and tell them when they feel better you want to discuss the situation with them. If you are the cause of the anger, remove yourself from the offensive environment quickly and take a brisk walk. Remember, anger does not accomplish what you are trying to accomplish, it only serves to complicate matters.

Activate a different conversation in your mind. Most of us say what we do because our mind tells us what a person is thinking. So after you or your child have cooled off and had some ice-cream, something that makes your taste buds happy, constructively engage in a positive conversation in your mind. Tell yourself that you can control your mind. We are responsible for our thoughts and actions. Since negative thoughts can bring inappropriate actions, tell yourself pleasant thoughts about yourself. For a child, help distract their thoughts for the time being onto something else and promise to talk to them when they are feeling calmer.

Rest and Responsibility - Most angry moments occur when people are tired. Try and get appropriate amounts of rest. Sadly, most arguments happen at night and cause even more restlessness. Take responsibility for your actions.

"No matter how calmly you try to referee, parenting will eventually produce bizarre behavior, and I'm not talking about the kids."
Bill Cosby

Remember, anger does not accomplish what you are trying to accomplish, it only serves to complicate matters.

Things Not To Do
- Do not use drugs
- Do not use alcohol
- Do not use other destructive means for a temporary fix to problems because they will temporarily numb your brain and make you unable to make rational choices; and then, when you are not under the influence, the situation will have worsened.

Things To Do
Find ways of relieving tension on a daily basis such as:
- Physical work
- Walking
- Running

"The rose turned into liquid blood, flowing down the stem completely covering each thorn."

Hobbies that involve physical activities help your blood pressure and help to relieve tension. Also, spiritual exercise helps a person relieve tension by getting their focus off their problems and on to God. Following the Biblical technique of rest, which includes daily prayer and devotion, will go a long way toward relieving daily tension as well.

Practice Forgiving
<u>A story on forgiveness</u>

One night during a church service, the Pastor asked the congregation to turn around and pray for the person behind them. As it turned out, behind me was a couple who suffered an abusive relationship. I asked God to help me pray with this couple, for I had no strength in myself. "What do you see?" I heard my Savior ask. A beautiful rose came before my eyes. Then He showed me a cross and said, "What do you see?" "A cross," I answered. He tenderly guided my eyes and mind. "What do you think of when you look at the cross?" He prodded. "Do you think of the power of the cross or the pain?" "I think of the power," I said. At that precise moment, I again saw the rose, but now its petals flowed like liquid blood and ran down the stem covering each thorn. In a strong voice, I heard Him say, "When you pray for that couple, think of the power of my blood. Not the pain, but the power. There is nothing my blood will not wash away." My breath went away. I knew that He was saying, "Glenda, I am the Rose of Sharon, the only rose without a thorn." In this life there will be pain, but look to the power of the blood and you will overcome the pain and know the power of forgiveness.
If Jesus can forgive after all He went through to gain power over sin, then I can continue to seek to know this forgiving power. It is a choice that we must willfully choose. I choose to forgive and act on purpose.

Only
one way to
maintain a
happy life...
Say,
"I forgive!"

Kite Kit Toolbox:

Vocabulary Toolbox for Chapter 6
Understanding Discipline

- **Stress**
- **Anger**
- **Control**
- **Consequence**
- **Manage**

Stress: Is tension from mental, emotional, physical, or spiritual source. Stress comes from not releasing tension on a daily basis.

Anger: A defensive mechanism that energizes your body when given certain signals, used to express strong feeling, disrupts thinking ability; unbridled produces inappropriate behavior rage, yelling, violent slapping, hitting, or throwing things.

Control: Management of a situation by making appropriate choices.

Consequence: The result of a decision or indecision

Manage: Take control of in an objective way

☆ Star Talk

Words, whether positive or negative, up-lifting or cursing, will fill our children's word reservoir and become the shaping tools for character, forming the core of their thought processes.

Family Appreciation (Life Styles)

Your lifestyle is in brief the way you live. Family traditions are good because they establish more than a meeting time. They help us understand our heritage and who we are. Some things are better "felt than telt."

Building a Healthy Environment

No matter the arrangement, first time marriage, blended families or single, the same principles must be applied. Building a healthy environment should be taking an interest in making the home a haven of rest. There needs to be an order of respect and cleanliness, inside and outside, so the children will not be ashamed to have friends over, no matter how humble the abode. Also, it speaks of the attitude of the home. It is up to the parents, especially the mother to set the mood for the environment of the home. Happy faces are the sign of a healthy environment. It takes a lot of effort to keep a cheery face, especially during the night feedings, etc. But it also sets the mood for happiness in the house. A smile in the morning creates a loving, nurturing mood for a great day.

The morning mood is critical for the rest of the day. Happy moments, make happy days. Happy days turn to happy weeks. Happy weeks turn to happy years. Pretty soon there are more happy ones than sad ones, and then it will be worth every effort you made.

Building respect for each other makes a safe cove of love where the best is possible for everyone. If this section alone was the only section I could write, it would be the most important for your children's well being. The greatest thing dad and mom can do for their children is to be kind to each other and work at making each person look good to the other members of the family. Agree to work out the issues in the bedroom or in privacy elsewhere away from the children. This might be very hard at times but it can be done. Over the years, my husband and I have done this. I know how hard it is to keep yourself together until you can discuss matters privately. You may not be 100% each time, but just because you blow it one time, do not give up. Ask forgiveness, and go on.

When Daddy Comes Home

There is no better reward for a dad than to hear joyous sounds in the house scurrying to meet his arrival. All day long the anxiousness of mom knowing that dad will be coming, to share their lives together from the responsibilities to the joys helps her get through the long days. Little noses press against the window many times during the day and at last the car turns into the driveway. The moment has arrived. With this kind of mutual anticipation, dad enters a cove of happiness. After dad greets the children and his wife, it is a good idea if he is given a little time for himself and his wife before dinner. I usually had the children continue with what they were doing for about ten minutes after dad told them hello. This picture is not possible if mom does not set it up. According to Proverbs, the wise lady builds up her house. As dad builds blessings, mom is building the inside trust by communicating wonderful things about dad. The children learn that mom and dad work hard all for each other. The messages are transferred by visual interaction of sounds and joy. Soon the children will move into higher stages of life where they need dad and mom's guidance in a greater way. If there are any loop holes where dad and mom are not together, the children are the first to know. When dad and mom are not together on main issues after marriage, having children further complicates the situation; it does not usually bring them together.

Family traditions are good for they establish more than a meeting time, they help us understand our heritage and who we are. "Some things are better felt than 'telt'".

Dad,
Over the years your toolbox has gotten heavy... heavy with memories. Shiny. Timeworn. Each perfect in its own way... Memories of things set right, of a world where two hands and a good heart still make a difference. Thank you for being the best.

Love your buddy, Joel

DAILY TRADITIONS ~ Daily Shine

(Styles of starting and ending the day.) One suggestion is to start the day with the family eating a breakfast together and end it with a wrap-up time. Set the stage according to the age of your children. The old adage says, "The family who eats together stays together." Another adage says, "The family who prays together stays together." Both of these are becoming outdated and almost obsolete, and so are the families who are intact. Having a devotional book and a Bible always on the table that contain short, mini-stories and Scriptures helps to fill everyone's pockets with stars for the day.

Mealtime

The happiest memories can be that of families gathered around their table. Setting the table nicely is a memory that most children cherish later in life. When we first came to the East Coast, I thought the sun never shined here. It seemed gray clouds appeared from December to April. After calling our aunt, Janet Trout, and seeking her advice, we began lighting candles. Since then, we have bought many candles. The fire in the center of the table brightens the world outside and keeps our hearts warm inside.

Conversations should be in unity at the table. Try connecting with each child and mate. "How was your day? Great! Fantastic! You are a hard worker." Use meal time to build. The goal is not to embarrass anyone by correcting them at the table. Otherwise, mealtime will become a challenge. For instance, depending on the child's age, you should let them know what is acceptable and unacceptable behavior at the table. (Do this at a time other than mealtime.) Mealtime should take place in a relaxed atmosphere but also be structured enough that conversations can flow while everyone is together.

Building Security

Parents need to use a private area with the doors closed for issues that will vary in opinions. The best gift you can give your child is love and respect for each other. I believe this is critical for a child's security. When parents do not hold back information from each other and are together on issues, a trust is built for parents and children. Trust for each other is something that children can sense like smelling bacon cooking in the kitchen. Then, as the child grows and you deal with issues like dating, curfews, etc., the hedge is already in place. This bond will keep children from playing the parents against each other. It will help the parents in their marriage. They will know the other parent is not going to be the nicey uncle with the ice-cream and themselves the sour pickle with the prickles. After working with families for more than 30 years, I have seen time and time again where this principle worked. I have watched with heartbreak, also, the times where parent after parent did not work together, and it was just a matter of time before their family completely broke up.

Trust

Build trust by being consistent and doing what you say. Trust is also built by being there. Children have a built in sense to want to trust their parents. I will never forget one instance where a child was told, "I will buy a particular instrument for you to learn." I will never forget how his eyes sparkled. Sadly, the parent never followed through. Unfortunately, the same parent never followed through about many things. The child innocently believed at first. Now the trust is completely broken in their relationship, and it has carried over bitterly in all other relationships as well.

Computers

The safest way to have a computer with the internet in the house is to keep it in the family room. There should not be any reason to have it elsewhere. Even if you are a family where there is only one child, the safest environment is to keep the internet in a place where you constantly monitor what your child is viewing. Would you allow a tiger in your house? No, you may say; yet something just as destructive is in your house when you do not have control over what goes on over the internet. Parents, please note, have you ever noticed the games your child is playing on the internet? Is it a desensitizer to words such as death, killing, and blood? Watch for these. The graphics are more than you will appreciate. Why do some think it is okay to own a game, and yet agree hands up, they do not want that same horror acted out in their house?

TV and Videos

The same is true for videos and TV. Educators, teachers, and parents all agree children spend too much time in front of the TV. Parents Action for Children report by current estimates, the average American child between the ages of two and eighteen spends almost six hours per day with electronic media. Television viewing accounts for well over half of that time. Sixty percent of kids ages 8-16 have a TV in their bedroom. The number of hours spent watching television is linked to lower performance in school, increased aggression, and obesity in children. High levels of Internet use are associated with lower communication skills and increased depression and loneliness. TV shows designed for children are five to six times more violent than adult shows. Someone needs to control the screens with an average of 20 to 25 violent acts per hour on Saturday morning kids' shows (Parents'Action for Children- Hitting the Off Button, 2). http:// www.parentsaction.org/learn/features/hittingtheoffbutton/

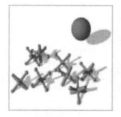

Toys and Games

We must guard the toys our children play with. I was appalled as my married daughter, Cherie, and her husband, Greg, related to me the new toys sold in some of the toy stores. The game, Dungeons and Dragons, which has been around a long time, gets you inside the person and do what they do: kill etc. While trying to find the educational game 'Leap Frog', they came across a computer game where you actually partake the blood of others in the game. This sounds gross, but these games are found in our local malls.

Teaching violence is not an accepted behavior and is becoming more difficult to control in our society. It seems you cannot buy a movie without some kind of violence. Children and teens will reproduce what they see. We must guard our children's attitude toward adults by supervising them very closely and observing their facial expressions. We cannot wait until they begin to speak disrespectfully before we do something about it. Consistant observation that will not contend for negative expressions will stop them before they grow to words and then actions.

What can we do about media culture and it's effect? Keep the computer in a family room. Do not allow a TV in each bedroom. Become media-wise by visiting Dr. Dobson's Focus on the Family website (www.family. org). Review games and movies before allowing your children or teens permission to purchase and use these games at home.

Going To Church

Although marriage is critical to the health of the family and the nation, regular worship of God is critical to the health of marriage and has many other desirable outcomes. There is greater degeneration in homes where there are no church goers. Going to church is not the most popular thing for young couples to do. Working hard all week many times will cause people to feel they deserve Sundays for themselves. However, the whole reason for this book is to help parents look boldly at the priorities in their lives and see what needs to be done to keep their purpose in focus. I once heard the story of a couple who visited the president of the United States. They related to him their belief that parents should not influence children concerning religion. So they did not bring their own children to church since this might influence them in an uncomfortable way. They went on to say that when their children became older, they could make up their own minds. Later, they asked to see the president's garden, and he politely led them to an open gateway. On one side of the garden was a patch of neglected weeds. "Oh, my," said the visitor, "This is nothing but weeds." "Yes," replied the president. "I did not want to influence the ground in this patch; therefore, this is what it produced." When parents lead the way to church in attendance, support, and participation, they will have the blessings of Abraham (that from him all the families of the earth shall be blessed).

The 10 Blessings of Church Attendance
1.   I worship God at church.
2.   I find fulfillment and purpose at church.
3.   I find salvation at church (an eternal value).
4.   My child is dedicated and finds salvation at church.
5.   I gain friendship at church.
6.   My children gain friends from the church.
7.   My child will marry at the church.
8.   My grandchildren will be dedicated at the church.
9.   I can give to something that will have eternal value.
10.   I hope my funeral will be at a church.
         It is never too late to start, even if your children are grown.
         Each new day is a golden new day of hope. Start today.

Star Talk ☆

Celebrate Your Child's Star Shine
Building a close relationship and self-esteem in your child is critical prior to the dating age. For starters, events such as birthdays, recitals, rehearsals, and anytime you are doing something special with your child, is a star-shining time. Birthday memories at the 12th birthday have been used by some as an age book-mark, representing the acknowledgement that you are aware your child is making changes. Some call this "The Blessing Birthday".

College Choices

Choosing which college your children will attend can be exasperating. Here are a few basic guidelines which may help you. If you live near quality universities and colleges where your children can commute, you are really blessed. As pastor of our church, my husband can no longer validate advising young people to go away to a college. Co-ed dormitories and Godless campuses impose lifestyles that are not safe or conducive to maintaining spiritual values. We think it is advisable to attend a nearby college, especially the first years of college. The risks otherwise are appalling. However, as parents, please seek the advice of Godly pastors and leadership.

The Blessing Birthday

When your child has a blessing birthday, you should invite a minister, a special friend, or the child's mentor to the party. If your child does not have a mentor, this is a good age to choose one (someone who is old enough to serve as a role-model and reinforce your same values). You may have a candlelight dinner at home, or go out. Create a table of their life accomplishments, gather the best pictures, and place a shining cloth under them. Surround their cake table with fun pictures; being creative is the key. Go for it! Let your child be on display. Spotlight their talent and leadership skills. Invest in combining pictures on a CD or video and have them playing in the background: school plays, church presentations, awards, recitals, etc. All this says, "I love you, and it's your time to shine, Baby." Make sure you take lots of pictures.

After the meal, a blessing prayer should be prayed by the the parents.

Sample Prayer:

Dear God,

I remember when my child,_____(Child's Name), was born. You saw him before he was born in the depths of the earth where his parts were formed. You have meant good for his life and not evil. He was the most beautiful baby I had ever seen. He fills our lives with so much joy. Now, Father, as you have so faithfully given him to us, we have given him back to You since birth. Once again we renew that commitment at this age of 12, as we acknowledge he is passing through another important phase of growth. Please take his life and mold it, and help him to always be a true servant of God by loving others as You have. Help him to be honest in all things, kind, and forgiving even as You forgive him. He is Yours, Father, his talents, his music, his voice, his hands, his feet. Please guide them in all Your ways and direct his steps even as You said in Your Word, "the steps of the righteous are ordered of the Lord."

Scrap booking

Many creative memory books are available on the market. There are even ways you can do this with the family and create extra income. Have fun putting your favorite memory spots together. Then you will be ready for the next celebration with a scrapbook journal in hand.

A Christmas Tradition

We use this special time of the year to remember our convictions, spiritual beliefs and the wonder of the birth of Jesus Christ. After dinner we bask by a glowing fire where each family member shares their heart of love for each other and the source of love, Jesus Christ. This is a great way to celebrate with our families, giving our children roots and special memories. On Christmas Eve, we keep a special time for our immediate family and use this time for memories with just our children. We usually have party foods on Christmas Eve: chicken salad with grapes, apples, and chopped pecans, eggnog, and other festive foods. We save the dressing and trimmings for Christmas Day when our extended family come. Aunts, uncles, and cousins arrive, bringing with them special Christmas dishes. My contribution is the cornbread dressing, a unique blend of recipes from my mother, Ollie Brock, and mother-in law, Bethel Andrus (Recipe below). For 28 years, we traveled south around 1,700 miles to Louisiana, but now my mother, two sisters and their families, and a niece and her sons are all in Delaware. What a huge family gathering the Lord has blessed me with. One of the very special highlights of the holiday season has been my husband's family, Bro. and Sis. Trout, visiting us.

Thanksgiving Dressing
Glenda Andrus

5	Boxes of Jiffy cornbread mix (bake separately)
5	Boiled eggs
2 lbs	Bob Evans Sausage, (browned) (1 lb can be original and 1 lb hot)
	Broth off of ham or turkey
2 lbs	Hamburger Meat (browned)
1	Large bag of Pecans (chopped)
1	Bell pepper
	Green onions
1	White onion
5	Wyler Bouillon Cubes (melted)

Saute bell peppers, green onions, & white onions, then combine with other ingredients in a large roasting oven. Bake about 30 - 45 minutes on 375. Garnish with paprika and pecans (Serves around 15 people.)

Stand   **T**ogether   **A**bilities   **R**esponsibilities   **S**tars for Ever
Where and When Do We Teach STARS Values for a Lifetime?

When our youngest child and son, Joel, was 13, he began taking bass lessons about 30 miles from our home. We made this decision knowing the drive and time would have to be considered. However, this decision proved to be one of the best in many ways. First of all, it became a time of bonding for Joel and his dad, since his dad usually drove him to class. Second, it furnished the time needed to do some heart teaching.

Teaching doesn't always need to be classroom style. Some of the best lessons are the ones that flow from the heart. This is what happened on Thursday evenings on the way to bass lessons. We bought the book, *Plants Grow Up*, teaching the nine fruits of the Spirit. We highly recommend this book by Pam Forster (1995). It provided some of the best teaching we have given our children. Children should be taught that only God can really fill their cups to overflowing. That is why we surround our lives with church and Godly living. There is a space in our heart that only God can fill. The only way He can fill it is if we are around His character and learn about Him. A great bond results from teaching these lessons to your children. Sometimes we all have been guilty of thinking, that we will just let the church teach these virtues. However, the time spent in positive teaching and talking about these virtues will save grief in years to come.

Passing on Stars – By Envisioning

When Jesus asked, "Has anyone any food?" Could it be that He saw the possibilities of stars instead of just dirty feet and sandals? Could it be someone had put something in that basket that said, "If you can get close enough to Jesus, the Miracle Man, do it." The little boy did, and God put stars in his lunch that day; stars that shined from his generation to ours today. Somebody knew how to pass on a blessing. Somebody was more interested in that little boy's heart than his lunch box. This is passing on the blessing.

I once heard a favorite heroine of mine, Joan Ewing, say these words, "What if more adults were concerned about finding crowns in their closets instead of dirty socks and tennis shoes. Would there be more kings?" If we looked behind the dirty socks and their old worn out sneakers, we might see a sling shot and 5 stones. Now just what are they doing with those? Could it be a giant killer lives in your house? Could it be, if you nurtured the good, you would bring out the David who would slay the giants of darkness and apathy that are overtaking our youth? If we would not only construct charts for academics and brushing teeth, but also for kindness, smiles, respect, helping our neighbors, etc. perhaps then we would definitely raise giant killers. They would never lack for self-esteem if they were shining in their neighborhood and at the senior center. Talk about giving them security. There could be no better security than instruments playing and voices singing. Stars are shining tonight.

Imagine

Imagine your child reaching his hand inside his lunch bag for a sandwich and pulling out a star. Actually, that is exactly what happened to the little boy with the five loaves of bread and three fish. He, no doubt, had followed Jesus day after day. His mother had prepared his lunch before, but today he found a star. Andrew, said, "I have nothing here but a little boy's lunch." And Jesus took it, broke it, and blessed it. It was enough to feed the multitude and have 12 full baskets left over.

I like to think the little boy's mother had prayed over his lunch that day as she had so many times before. I like to think that because she prayed, he was bold enough to tell Andrew, "Here, I have a lunch".

I don't think it mattered if the lunch box had cool colors and a nifty-fifty purple ice-cooler inside. More than likely, it was just a basket with a woven cloth protecting the precious lunch. It was not the name brand on the basket that made the difference but the heart brand of the one who had prepared it.

To think this child was at the right place at the right time, with his Hero, Jesus, was more than a mere coincidence. This child was about to see his usual lunch turned into a miracle... fish, bread, and the miraculous. Who would have dreamed it? Thousands would be fed that day, but countless thousands thereafter! Stars forevermore.

The influence of your child's heroes and friends has everything to do with their future. Perhaps, if more parents were concerned about where their child was going and the company they were keeping, I believe there would still be the bread and the blessing. Here are some Stars we can slip into our children's baskets; and one day when they are near enough to Jesus, He will take what our children have, break it, bless it, and feed thousands.

Kite Talk: Flying over peer pressure is almost impossible, unless the string is tight!

Star Talk

Who Is Your Child's Favorite Hero? If you can get your child to his favorite hero, will that hero multiply what he has or take away his substance? The influence of your child's heroes and friends has everything to do with their future.

Words, whether positive or negative, up-lifting or cursing, will fill our children's word reservoir and become the tools shaping their character and forming the core of their thought processes.

Stars In Their Ears

If we are to instill truths and virtues about life and others, we must guard what our children hear. Sometimes we guard what goes into their lunch boxes perhaps a little more carefully than what goes into their ears and minds. What their brain filters and what debris is left on the floor of their heart and mind is the information I am speaking of. Words, whether positive or negative, up-lifting or cursing, will fill our children's word reservoir and become the tools shaping their character and forming the core of their thought processes. Because of the power of negative words, we virtually have the ability to destroy others.

For instance, a phone call; someone chatting with you about a sensitive situation. It is your job to keep the adults in your children's life free to be a rope of safety they might one day need. Someday your child might need the kindness that only another adult can offer. If you have destroyed their confidence in that adult by your careless tongue, it is as if you have cut the ropes that could bring your child back to safe harbor.

Case Protecting Your Child's Mind From the Offences of Adults

Perhaps you receive a phone call from a person who wishes to discuss an incident concerning someone else. You may respond, "Thank you, Mrs. X, for giving me the trust you have intended. However, now is probably not a good time. I will need to get in touch with you later concerning this issue. Thank you. Good bye." Postpone the conversation until you can have it in private, out of your children's hearing.

Case A:

Mother, I don't appreciate Mrs. Albright coming to me and telling Sue to come home directly after the party was over. I had planned to ride around a little while with her. Now that blows my plans.

Mother's Incorrect Response:

Ann, darling, you are absolutely right. She had no business interfering with your plans. After all, you should know what you want to do; and besides that, she and Bro. Albright are always interfering with somebody's plans. They ought to take care of their own problems. Did you see the look he gave her when she told him that she was expecting him to help her carry the food into the hall? So don't worry, Darling, everyone knows they are the ones having the problem, not you.

Mother's Correct Response:

Ann, I know you had some plans and you are disappointed; however, Mrs. Albright is Susie's mother, and she knows what is best for her child. One thing for sure, Mrs. Albright is not doing this to hurt you. Perhaps you can ask Alice, and she will still be allowed. If not, as we also know, God knows best. Perhaps we can have a little more time together ourselves.

If further guidance is needed: Now Ann, I know you are disappointed; but I will not allow inappropriate behavior. You have been faced with a disappointment, not a permanent liability, and you have this option. Will you accept this cheerfully or do you need further instructions with a disciplining measure?

Stars In Thought and Speech
Protecting Your Child Against Harboring Thoughts Against Others

Perhaps a child has been unkind or thoughtless in some deed or action. Wouldn't it be better to offer a negotiated thought than to become critical of every child that is in contact with your child? For instance, a typical scenario may be:

Sally: (eyes all red and face flushed) Mother, I have been so embarrassed. You know Lacy Emerald. She has totally destroyed my image to everyone.

Mother: (wrong response; taking child into embrace) Tell Mother what that rude child has done this time? Doesn't she know who she is fooling around with?

Sally: Oh, Mother, I can't stand it. She looked at me with her glaring stare and said, "What is it to you?" I was just listening to her tell Leanne why John isn't coming over Friday night.

Mother: (correct response) Now, Sally, while this must have been embarrassing, you must remember everyone needs a chance to explain. Don't read into a situation. The Bible teaches us to treat everyone as you would want to be treated. Perhaps Lacy Emerald will explain her behavior tonight. It is pleasing to God for all to dwell in unity.

Appropriate Behavior In Speech

Speech should 'become' a person in subject and manner. Always choosing far-out subjects to debate sets a person apart, not in a good sense of the word, and displays an insecure person. A leader-type character looks for subjects that most people will agree upon, and the conversation will flow. Becoming emphatic, harsh, or dogmatic only illustrates a need for control and actually an immaturity on the part of the speaker. It is thoughtful to stay away from argumentative subjects. One who always puts down others to emphasize his beliefs is another type of insecure person. A leader who is secure in his own beliefs and convictions should not need to make negative remarks openly about others. Doing so is beneath their dignity and value of life.

If you find yourself around someone who continues to bring down the conversation and talk about crude subjects, try to take leadership by changing the subject to something you know will guide the conversation back on course. If this doesn't work, politely dismiss yourself so you will not be caught in a snare (Psalm 119:110; Proverbs 18:7). Webster's states that discretion is the quality of being discreet, being careful about what one does and says. Indiscreet people are not to be sought out and numbered among your close friends. "As a jewel of gold in a swine's snout, so is a fair woman which is without discretion" (Proverbs 11:22).

The following verses further demonstrate the value God's Word places on proper speech and Godly behavior:

Psalms 1:1-2 Blessed is the man that walketh not in the counsel of the ungodly, nor standeth in the way of sinners, nor sitteth in the seat of the scornful, but his delight is in the law of the Lord; and in his law doth he meditate day and night.

James 3:16 For where envying and strife is, there is confusion and every evil work.

II Thessalonians 3:14 And if any man obey not our word by this epistle, note that man, and have no company with him, that he may be ashamed.

I Thessalonians 5:12-13 And we beseech you, brethren, to know them which labor among you, and are over you in the Lord, and admonish you; And to esteem them very highly in love for their work's sake. And be at

peace among yourselves.

Finding Real Shine (Lessons From The Closet)

A closet, a place for keeping our clothing, a place of prayer, the place we stack things. Jesus said, a place of prayer.

Keeping life's purpose: Not as the Pharisee, but in your closet of prayer. While he was probably not telling everyone to get into a literal closet to pray, He was saying, "There are some areas that we keep stuff." You know the stuff in our lives that no one may really know is there. He is saying, "You have got to get in there to pray." Really that is where He sees us praying. We may be in a beautiful cathedral; but when we pray He sees us just the way we are, in the stuff. This stuff, from time to time, needs to be discarded. Either it doesn't fit any longer or we just plain don't need it. Here in our closet, the disarray can be overwhelming in real life and also in our spiritual life.

The best lesson children can learn about praying is hearing their parents pray for it tells them their parents really believe it works. I have so many memories of hearing my dad and mom praying. Both my husband's father and my own dad have gone on to be with the Lord, but we both remember the altars that marked their pathway of life. Without their prayers and our mothers prayers, we would not have wanted to dedicate our lives to God. Their example nurtured the desire inside of our hearts to find God for ourselves and helped to mold us into what we became. Since we have pastored in Delaware for 34 years, my husband, Royce, has made it a practice to go to the church everyday at 6:00 a.m. for his daily devotion. His steady plodding has been an anchor for our family and church. My devotion has been at home because of the care of the children. It really doesn't matter where your closet is as long as you find one. These daily devotions help us hold on to purpose and sets an example for our children. There are times prayer and faith in God are the only answer that take us through life.

I really don't believe we can mature as believers without prayer. We want our children to mature in their attitudes and spirit. Unless we become their examples, humbling ourselves in prayer, how can we teach them?

What a golden opportunity to teach lessons in finding stars, starting right in the closet. Once the stuff is cleared, our vision may expand past the bad attitude and stinking pride and the dirty socks and dirty sneakers. Instead of seeing just the junk, we may see the stars, stones, sling shots, and kings. Getting our vision cleared in our closet of prayer cleans out the old and prepares space for the new.

To My Momma and Daddy, You have given me wings and I'm soaring now... right into the arms of God. Thank you for praying for me. Your prayers feed the wind I'm flying into. You are my heroes!

Love,
Shiloh Joy

Kite Talk:
Evaluation for Chapter 6

1. Name five ways to identify burnout in an adult.

_____

2. Name five things to do for stress management for yourself.

_____

3. What is the S. T. A. R. method of managing anger.

_____

4. What are five symptoms of stress in children?

_____

5. What are 5 ways you can relieve stress in children?

_____

Notes

_____

_____

_____

_____

_____

_____

_____

_____

_____

_____

SHINE

PERSONAL MAPPING, PARENTING SHINE CHART, AND PARENTING PROMISES
FEATURING "HEAVEN'S ART GALLERY"

SHINE

PERSONAL MAPPING, PARENTING SHINE CHART, AND PARENTING PROMISES
FEATURING "HEAVEN'S ART GALLERY"

Painting With Light

Thomas Kinkade paints pictures of homes with "light" as his theme. The pictures he paints bring us all back to happy moments or wistful ones where we are basking in a glow of love all around us. I am a great fan of his portraits for I, too, share the belief of wanting to paint pictures of light.

As we come to the close of our parenting journey together, I truly want to thank you for allowing me to join you. It is my deep desire that you continue gathering stars of purpose for a lifetime and your big picture of life, like Kinkade's, keeps your home glowing forever. Now, it is your opportunity to turn the light on in your home. Hopefully, throughout your parenting kite flight you have refocused your parenting purpose, filled your pockets full of stars, and are now ready to bring home the shine.

Ready to Fly your Kite?

Congratulations! You have almost finished building your parenting kite. In chapter 1-4 we learned about our kite through fabric, sticks, and string. In the last three chapters, we added the final touch by connecting the train to our kite. This last attachment will help the kite remain in the air. As parents, the choices we make in our lifestyle determine our endurance level and how high and long we soar.

Your Personal "Shine"

This last chapter is designed to be a personal work-shop for each individual. Included is a Parenting Shine Profile and Evaluation Chart. By using these tools, you can easily spot daily and monthly soaring skills. By gathering the information from your completed "Kite- talk" evaluations at the end of each chapter, you have an indication of how high your parenting kite may be flying and also you are able to build your own personal shine profile; the Parenting Shine Chart. Fill in the blanks on the profile below. Remember no one is perfect, but we can all maximize our strengths and minimize our weaknesses to bring home the shine.
Happy Flying!

Kite Talk: Hopefully, through-out this parenting journey you have filled your pockets full of stars. Now you are ready to bring home the shine.

My Parenting Shine Profile
"Shine"

My name is _____

I am the Parent of, _____
This is my (1st, 2nd, 3rd) marriage. I know I have (little, some, much) baggage from previous life experience.
My best skills for parenting are _____, My negatives are _____
Because of certain life situations, which could influence my children, I must work hard to keep the relationships _____

In my big picture of life, I value_____first , and _____second.

The four growth areas of my own self are _____ , _____,

_____ , and _____. I am doing (excellent, well, average, poor, or below average) in taking care of these areas.

My personal talent is _____I strive hard to manage my time so I can fulfill this area. (Yes… NO… Sometimes)

My basic personality is _____and _____

My personality strengths are _____and _____

My personality weaknesses are_____and _____

My best parenting style is _____ , although I struggle hard not to become

_____.

I communicate best by _____and I work hard to _____
_____, for this is not my natural skill.

I would really love to use up words for flying my parenting kite. These are my favorite

up-words_____ , _____ , _____ ,

The down words_____ , _____ , _____ , _____ , I am working hard not to use.

They cause a_____down draft.

However, because I am a Bee-liever and better than a bumblebee, I know I can become a parent who flies my parenting kite high into the skies of possibilities. I believe my child has talents, and I will work hard to develop them by becoming a _____ of time.

My best disciplining style is_____, but (many times, most of the time,

often, seldom) I become angry and _____ at my child.

If my life is balanced in these four areas_____ , _____ ,

_____ , _____ my parenting kite has a better chance of staying in the air.

_____fabric is the best of all for flying endurance, and reaching the most possibilities of helping my child.

I will not bump my head on the daily grind, for there is no ceiling for high flyers. I am a Bee-liever, and I will practice love words, manage my time, overcome personal baggage by envisioning the possibilities of my child, help manage his time, and keep flying until his talents and character become shining stars which warm all of those around.

Kite Talk:
A Review

Chapter 1: Seeing the Big Picture
- Standing on values
- Finding our purpose
- Establishing our priorities
- Strategizing various options

Chapter 2: Together Building Relationships
- Working toward building our relationships
- Evaluating our relationship with God, family, others
- Needing love to bond relationships
- Practicing forgiveness to maintain relationships
- Identifying our personality styles to understand our strengths and weaknesses
- Building enduring relationships by first understanding ourselves

Chapter 3: Abilities, Academics, Talents, and Time
- Bringing out the best in talent, character, and academics
- Using the SHINE technique
- Building your child's character
- Finding your child's talents
- Developing your child's gifts
- Strengthening your child's academics
- Using the child's profile to understand your child, keeping progress moving by the "Shine" plan
- Managing time wisely

Chapter 4: Raising Kites and Kids
- Understanding discipline
- The "Shine Motivational Plan"
- Finding a level of respect functioning in your home

Chapter 5: Star Dust
- Training a prince and princess
- Managing anger and stress
- Dating tips and manners
- Tackling hard-to-address issues

Chapter 6: Flying Techniques
- Planning for action
- Instilling leadership values
- Building a healthy environment
- Envisioning the total outcome
- Keeping our closets clean

Chapter7: Shine
- Creating your personal parenting profile
- Mapping your parenting progress

Personal Shine Mapping Chart

The chart below is to serve as an indicator at a glance of how well you are shining and how high your parenting kite is flying. It shows where you can dust the shine for a brighter glow. Have fun and always keep the Shine at Home the brightest. Star techniques can help you turn the lights on all around and paint glowing pictures of love shine.

Personal Shine Mapping Chart (Sample)

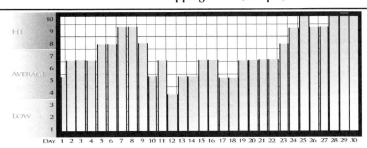

Personal Shine Mapping Chart (Monthly)

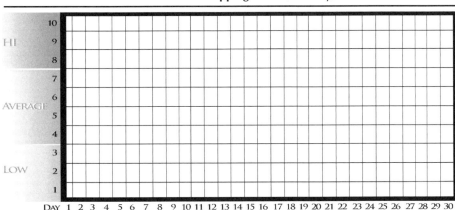

Give yourself 1 point for low score and 10 points for a high score.

All of the characteristics for the best possible Shining parenting profile are discussed in the previous chapters of this book. After carefully reading the chapters, you can, by honest evaluation, build your personal shine profile by giving yourself one point in the areas in which you reach the best shine. Add up your total score and place on Profile Shine Chart daily for a monthly glance at how well you are bringing home the shine! You can color your bar graphs for a better view.

- Parenting Style - Balanced
- Time Manager by having him work on talent one hour a day … in segments or whole
- Discipline System… Train by example; teach character.. And discipline with respect and con sequences.
- Shine Character - Building Bee-lieving character traits; I am better than a bumblebee I can fly
- Using my personal shine Profile to keep me flying

- Staying on track of Big Picture
- Nurturing Healthy Self
- Nurturing healthy relationships attachments, bonding, - up communication
- Personality Style, using your best strengths
- Communication style; active listening
- Using up words and Filling love tanks

Saying Good-bye is never easy for me. I can remember the long trips to Louisiana and how we would stand lingering not wanting to leave our parents. Now, I feel the tug again. I can remember trying to distract the children with fun things, while trying to hold back the tears myself. You and I have had quite a time on this parenting journey yet, there seems to be so many important things I should have said. However, I know when it really comes to living, you will have to make the choice. May I gently put my arms around you and say, I have confidence that you will make the right choices as you go on into the different seasons of your life. So instead of saying, "Good-bye," …for fun,

"Let's Go Fly A Kite!"

1. First of all look for a large opening. (Avoid hang-ups)

2. Keep a firm footing. (Build upon values that last)

3. Make sure your kite is attached securely. (Relationships can build bridges or gaps)

4. Run to get your kite in the air. (Remember not to fly your kite into a storm, just wait until it passes)

5. Run to keep your kite in the air. (Keep moving through life with the "Shine" in mind)

6. I bee-lieve in you! You will catch some parenting stars!

7. God keep you until we meet again.

Heaven's Art Gallery

By Harrison Woodard

One night I dreamed I was standing with Jesus in front
of a beautiful museum in heaven.
"Let's go inside," said Jesus. "I want to show you something."
Adorning the walls were paintings, all masterpieces.
Jesus explained that each one represents one human life.
Every painting in the museum was abounding with
love, grace, peace and passion.
I was overwhelmed with joy as I gazed at each one.
They all moved me deeply and I was aware of
everything lacking in my life.
I asked Jesus, "Who could paint such things of beauty?
Did you or the angels make these?
Surely, no human could create such perfection."
Jesus smiled, "These were all created by God's children."
"How?" I asked. "It just isn't possible."
"With God's help, anything is possible," said Jesus.
"Ordinary people who submitted their will to me created them.
Whenever a heart is truly given to me in every way,
that person's life will become a masterpiece.
Pride, selfishness, fear, greed, doubt, and unbelief will corrupt their painting.
But someone who loves me with all of his or her spirit, mind, and body
will live a life worthy of display."

We walked around the gallery admiring all the lives portrayed.
After a while, Jesus said that was all there was to see here.
But I protested, "Surely there is more to see, Lord.
For you've shown me only a few." Jesus said, "Yes, there is more."
He led me to the back of the museum and out into a massive warehouse.
Stacked on pallets and laying in heaps on the floor were millions of paintings.
I looked at a few and was disappointed. They were so poorly done.
Some were torn, some were patched, and still others lay unfinished.
"What is this Lord?" I asked. "Surely these don't belong here?"
"Yes my son, they do," said Jesus. "For each one represents a
precious life in progress."
"But they are such pitiful paintings.
Hardly worthy of a museum like this," I argued.
"Yes, you are correct they are not worthy," explained Jesus.
"But my Father is very patient. Each person's life has a chance
to become a masterpiece. All these people as long as they live,
can still see their life displayed in heaven's art gallery."

"How can this be?" I asked. "Surely not through their own efforts."
"No, they will never do it on their own.
They need only ask me and I will help," said Jesus.
I timidly asked, "What will happen if they never ask?"
We walked to the very back of the warehouse and Jesus opened the doors.
Off in the distance I saw stacks and stacks of paintings burning in massive piles.
I turned to Jesus and there were tears on his cheek.
"All these tried it on their own. Actors & athletes,
businessmen & butchers, executives & educators, preachers &
politicians, moms & dads, rich & poor, foolish & wise
– they are all here. As long as people keep trying under their
own strength they will never be good enough.
And their canvas will be thrown into the fire –
never to be admired. What a terrible waste," sighed Jesus.
I wept with him. It was such a tragic site.
Jesus closed the doors and we walked back into the warehouse.

I asked, "Lord is there hope for me?" Jesus smiled, "Yes! Follow me."
We walked into a small room that was empty except for a blank
canvas sitting on an easel. "What is this?" I asked.
"This canvas represents your life after it has been washed
cleaned with my blood," said Jesus.
I marveled at how beautiful it was. There was not one blemish or imperfection
anywhere on my canvas. Jesus handed me a brush and paint.
"Make it whatever you wish," said Jesus
I stood there for several minutes imagining all the things I could paint.
I realized that I could do nothing that would ever be good
enough for heaven's art gallery.
"Lord, I want to create a masterpiece, but I just can't."
Disappointed, I handed the brush back to Jesus, but he stopped me.
Wrapping his hand around the brush in my hand
and putting his arm around me he said,
"Let's make it together."

Stars That Shine Forever
Promise Stars
Hebrew Account of Promises, which are for those who would like to claim them for their children.

Train up a child in the way he should go: and when he is old, he shall not depart from it. (Proverbs 22:6)

Every good gift and every perfect gift is from above, and cometh down from the Father of lights... (James 1:17)

Before I formed thee in the belly I knew thee; and before thou camest forth out of the womb I sanctified thee, and I ordained thee a prophet unto the nations (Jeremiah 1:5)

Lo, children are an heritage from the Lord: and the fruit of the womb is his reward. As arrows are in the hand of a mighty man: so are the children of the youth. Happy is the man who has his quiver full of them. (Psalm 127: 3-5)

I will praise thee; for I am fearfully and wonderfully made: Marvelous are thy works; and that my soul knoweth right well. My substance was not hid from thee, when I was made in secret, and curiously wrought in the lowest parts of the earth. Thine eyes did see my substance, yet being unperfect; and in thy book all my members were written, which in continuance were fashioned, when as yet there was none of them. How precious also are thy thoughts unto me, Oh God! How great is the sum of them! If I should count them, they are more in number than the sand: When I awake, I am still with thee. (Psalms 139: 14-18)

Fight the good fight of faith, lay hold on eternal life, whereunto thou art also called, and hast professed a good profession before many witnesses. (I Timothy 6:12)

And this is the confidence that we have in Him, that, if we ask any thing according to His will, He heareth us: ...whatsoever we ask, we know that we have the petitions that we desired of him. (I John 5:14-15)

If ye shall ask anything in my name, I will do it. (John 14:14)

And ye shall know the truth, and the truth shall make you free. (John 8:32)

Salvation;
If we confess our sins, he is faithful and just to forgive us our sins, and to cleanse us from all unrighteousness. (I John 1:9)

...All things work together for good to them that love God, to them who are the called according to His purpose. (Romans 8:28)

My Supplier;
But my God shall supply all your need according to His riches in glory by Christ Jesus. (Philippians 4:19)

My Love;
For God hath not given us the spirit of fear; but of power, and of love, and of a sound mind. (II Timothy 1:7)

Faith;
...God hath dealt to every man the measure of faith. (Romans 12:3)

Greatness;
...Greater is He that is within you, than he that is in the world. (I John 4:4)

Triumph;
...God always causeth us to triumph in Christ. (II Corinthians 2:14)

Place of Care;
Cast thy burden upon the Lord, he shall sustain thee: He shall never suffer the righteous to be moved. (Psalms 55:22)

Be careful for nothing; but in everything by prayer and suplication with thanksgiving let your request be made known unto God. (Philippians 4:6)

Therefore I say unto you, Take no thought for your life, what ye shall eat, or what ye shall drink; nor yet for your body, what ye shall put on. Is not the life more than meat, and the body than raiment? Behold the fowls of the air: for they sow not, neither do they reap, nor gather into barns; yet your heavenly Father feedeth them. Are ye not much better than they? (Mathew 6: 25-27)

What shall we then say to these things? If God be for us, who can be against us? (Romans 8: 31)

APPENDIX i
RESOURCES FOR YOUR USE

Trends Showing Degeneration of Homes in American Society

Era of Time	Names	Attitude to Authority	Purpose
1900-1928	Victorian	Respectful	To earn enough for living.. and wished they had more education to get a better job
1930-1945	Depression Survivors	Endure Them	Taught children to seek education … to earn enough … to get education first
1946-1964	Boomers	Replace Them	Education first; Godless
1965- 1983	Groovers, Hippies-Yippies	Ignore Them	Decline of Homes
1984-2001	Millennial's	Choose Them	Job First; Home's degeneration

Chart idea taken from Tim Elmore, *Nurturing the Leader within Your Child (p. 77).*

Number one through five for qualifying a bonding and attaching time.
(five being the highest)

Bonding& Attachment Builders

- ___ Parents tend to child's needs
- ___ Routines
- ___ Feedings
- ___ Show affection to each other and baby
- ___ Talking, interacting
- ___ Attending church
- ___ Responsible parenting
- ___ Bathing, dressing
- ___ Committed to values
- ___ Happy environment

Bonding & Attachment Blockers

- ___ Both parents work and drop baby off at sitter
- ___ Parents fail to build consistent patterns or routines
- ___ No affection or interchange of affectionate wooing
- ___ Disconnection of emotion from child
- ___ Parents do not go to church
- ___ Quarreling
- ___ Harsh environment

172

A P P E N D I X i

Four Areas of Self-Examination

·Physical	Proper nutrition, rest, clothing, exercise,dental care, sight, hearing	Self Governing	Areas I need to improve (e.g. exercise 1 hour daily)
·Mental	Ability to think, rationalize, educate, rest, nurture understanding	Positive Thinking Self discipline Godliness	Take care of stress, Taking time for positive input (books, etc.), evaluate mental growth..
·Emotional	Care, the seat of understanding temperament, social interaction,self-actualization, self worth .	Self Governing	Understanding myself too, understand others, evaluate stress, find daily moments of rest
·Spiritual	Temperament, seat of self-actualization, values,standards of life etc. Moral consciousness	Self-governing mind Godliness growth	Daily devotions, prayer relationship, personal relationship with God

The Four Temperaments - Personality Evaluations

	Strengths	Traits	Weaknesses
·Sanguine	Joyful and Outward	Giver	Impulsive and Messy
·Phlegmatic	Patient and Peaceful	Quiet	Low Motivation and Inward
·Melancholy	Talented and Affectionate	Moody	Inward
·Choleric	Leader Type, Organizer	Strong Willed	Commanding and Low Tolerance

Personality Grid

Personality	Strengths & Emotions	Weaknesses	At Work
Sanguine	Joyful, makes home fun, people lover	Impulsive, brassy, forgetful, interrupts, angered easily, messy	Creative, energetic, catalyst for new jobs, storyteller, good host at parties
Phlegmatic	Calm, avoids conflicts, good under pressure, diplomat	Low-motivation, blank, mumbles, compromising	Patient, persistent, good job in routines
Choleric	Determined, exerts leadership, knows the right answer	Domineering, argumentative, tactless	Goal oriented, delegates, good salesman or leader,
Melancholy	Compassionate, self-sacrificing, deep feelers	Analytical, resentful, withdrawn, too sensitive, manipulator	Perfectionist, sees the problems, good musician, writer, etc.

Try the Personality Temperament Test for Fun

Place the number 1, 2, 3, 4, or 5 by each personality characteristic, with 5 being the strongest and 1 the weakest. Score and look at the personality grill to find your strongest temperament

·**Sanguine**	Socialize		Charmer		Impulsive
·**Phlegmatic**	Monotonous Jobs		Systematic		Very Laid Back
·**Choleric**	Good Salesmen		Strong willed		Can be domineering
·**Melancholy**	Servant Spirit		Compassionate		Whiner

A
P
P
E
N
D
I
X

i

A Grid for Parenting Blends

		Combinations of Personalities	Spirit Controlled
Sanguine Mom	Choleric Dad	Mom's joyfulness may irritate dad's goals, and loud arguments may result in front of children.	Dad needs to talk to mom and ask her to help him reach goals with children, and she needs to assess her responsibilities and comply.
Phlegmatic Mom	Choleric Dad	Mom's laid back nature and dad's lack of tact can cause phlegmatic mom to hide children's mistakes. This leads to disobedient children.	Mom needs to realize she is going to hinder children trusting them as parents. She needs to quit hiding and confront dad alone if need be and continue to discipline.
Choleric Mom	Phlegmatic Dad	Mom's goal-oriented nature can be mistaken for bossiness by dad and a resentful environment results for dad does not participate in disciplining.	Dad needs to become more alert, assess his duty and fulfill his role as dad. Mom needs to assess and rely upon dad.
Melancholy Mom	Sanguine Dad	Dad's fun, impulsive personality was fun in courtship, but now he grows angry quickly; and melancholy Mom can become depressed unless some help is given to direct dad to fulfill his responsibilities.	Mom needs to emphasize the need for dad to assess his responsibilities and assume his role. While he is fun, he needs to balance and assess his responsibility.

★ My Child's Shine Profile

Name: _____

Age: _____

Basic Personality Type: _____

Best Learning Style: _____

What you want them to excel in?

Academically _____

Character _____

Talent _____

In sports he/she likes _____

In music he/she would like to play _____

He/She likes to hum and sing with the music _____

He/She likes to speak _____

He/She loves poetry and likes to read _____

He/She enjoys crafts _____

Train and move forward by Door of Life Incentive Shine Plan
Blending natural (personal style) life incentives with consequences

Think Outside the Box.

How many boxes do you see?"
Please do not say 20. Look again, and notice the question,
"How many boxes do you see?"
One answer is 30, but another is 100.

If you look at a situation and think you will be succumbed by that situation, think again.

There are 100 reasons not to think there are only 16 squares above. There are many possibilities that can be achieved if we look beyond the obvious.

In chapter one, we dealt with parental baggage. Perhaps this is your third marriage and you have children from each. Perhaps this is your first and your child is only two years old. Whatever the case, remove all negative thoughts and go with me on a trip to the Bumble Bee Factory.

APPENDIX i

Official Kite Flyer Certificate

"Shine"

Member of the Bee Family

"I am better than a bumblebee"
I Bee- Lieve I CAN FLY!
This certificate, hereby certifies that,

(Parent's name) _____

agrees to the following:

_____

I _____ , agree that as of today

_____ (date), the parents of, _____,

_____ and _____,

agree to do as much as the bumblebee and overcome anything that
will keep me out of the air.
I agree to find at least one thing my child does well and promote his practice time

_____ , and day by day he will grow self-esteem.

He will grow character for I agree to train him in a particular life lesson such as

one hour on _____ each week.

His/Her self-esteem will flourish!

Signed _____
(kite flyer)

I am better than the bee!
This bee certificate is good for growing flyers, any shape, size, or color.
My child will grow in these areas - character, talent, and academics.
My pledge as a Bee Parent is to Bee there, to bee a model Bee, and Bee-lieve in my child.
I promise to bee a provider helping him/her to bee productive!

Pocket Full O' Stars Inc.

Sample Family Clock

 **6:30 a.m.**
Rise and shine,
wash up
and get dressed

 **4:00 p.m.**
Practice
instrument or
talent skill

 **7:00 a.m.**
Breakfast

4:30 p.m.
Start homework
study, etc.

 **7:20 a.m.**
Daily devotion,
prayer and Bible
reading (take turns
reading daily devotion
together)

5:00 p.m.
Dinner

7:30 a.m.
Children make
beds, morning
routine, get
dressed and
brush teeth

  **5:45 p.m.**
Do a few chores

8:00 a.m.
Children leave
for school

  **6:30 p.m.**
Finish any
unfinished task

3:30 p.m.
Children return
home; free time,
relax

  **7:00 p.m.**
Toddlers through
five years start on
night's routine -
story down time.
6-8 year olds can have
special time with family
and friends or extra cur-
ricular activities.

Official Bee-liever's
Certificate of Authenticity
Member of the Bee Family
"I am better than a bumblebee"
I Bee- Lieve I CAN FLY!
This certificate, hereby certifies that,

(Parent's name) _____

agrees to the following:

_____

I _____ , agree that as of today

_____ (date), the parents of, _____ ,

_____ and _____ ,

agree to do as much as the bumblebee and overcome anything that
will keep me out of the air.
I agree to find at least one thing my child does well and promote his practice time

_____ , and day by day he will grow self-esteem.
He will grow character for I agree to train him in a particular life lesson such as

one hour on _____ each week.

His/Her self-esteem will flourish!

Signed _____
(kite flyer)

I am better than the bee!
This bee certificate is good for growing flyers, any shape, size, or color.
My child will grow in these areas - character, talent, and academics.
My pledge as a Bee Parent is to Bee there, to bee a model Bee, and Bee-lieve in my child.
I promise to bee a provider helping him/her to bee productive!

Pocket Full O' Stars Inc.

APPENDIX i

Age	0-1	2-3	4-5	6-7
Molding and Shaping Temperament And Personality	Security, a child's basic security is gathered by their ability to decipher sensations and plan actions	Meal time should be pleasant: with healthy routines	Challenges of eating. BE CONSISTENT. Be firm, yet kind	Use meal time for practicing good manners and posi-tive self- image. However, if cor-rection needs to take place, try to play it down and do it at a different time
Nutrition - START it as early as 2-weeks start plac-ing a soft spoon on baby's tongue to help them get used to the feel. Some have found this training allows for spoon feedings as early as 3-4 weeks and helps transition	Routine feeding is the key… Wait at least 3-4 hrs. (too soon and baby will not eat or get satis-fied) toy distrac-tions and making noises helps baby eat.	Allow child to hold spoon as soon as he tries… keep encouraging. However, finger foods chicken sticks, fruit are favorites at this age.	Finicky eaters can be handled by say-ing, "Okay, if you do not want to eat your chicken sticks and you want snacks, that is fine. However, here is your chicken (etc.) When you decide to eat this then you can have your snack".	Using this time to play games such as describing picture cards. It could be a box of cards on table.
Changing Clothing Choosing etc.	When changing baby especially as they get older…hold leg firmly and let them know you are in control. Do not allow running from you when chang-ing diaper	Potty training can be done as early as child begins to walk and he begins to use a cup. There are videos and books on this subject. Stickers and awards are fun.	If your child is one that likes to choose his clothes, that is okay, but limit his choices. Place two shirts on the bed and let them choose between those articles.	Using this time to play games such as describing picture cards. It could be a box of cards on table.
Bathing Bedtime etc.		Children need space and time. As you allow them to bathe, use this time to prepare their mind for bedtime by saying, "When you finish your bath, we will have our story," or say, "It's nightime."		

Pocket Full O' Stars Inc.

181

Sample Information Sheet for Building Shine Profile

Age	Responsibility	Talent	Character	Incentive
2-3	Hygiene or skill	Music, art, craft	Obedience	Daily. Small treats or stickers
4-5	Hygiene or skill trash, make bed	Practice letters	Sharing	Big Friday McDonalds
6-8	Trash , makebed, clean sink vacuum (8)	Practice reading	Manners	A class they enjoy, sports, gym
9-11	Trash, mow yard,make bed and clean room	Practices on rental INSTRUMENT looking forward to own	Self Control	New instrument trumpet... etc.
12-15	Awake with alarm clock. Do all the above clean closet & help with kitchen chores	Owns instrument practice, recitals	Respect	Involve with extra curricular conferences, etc. driver's license
16-18	All the above Keep car washed	Continues practice, recitals	9 Characteristics listed in Chapter 5	Drive car College choices

Pocket Full O' Stars Inc.

A
P
P
E
N
D
I
X
i

Personal Shine Mapping Chart

The chart below is to serve you as an indicator at a glance of how well you are shining and how high your parenting kite is flying It shows you where you can dust the shine for a brighter glow. Have fun and always keep the Shine at Home the brightest. Star techniques can help you turn the lights on all around and paint glowing pictures of love shine.

Personal Shine Mapping Chart (Sample)

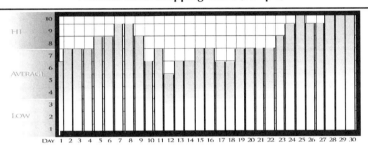

Personal Shine Mapping Chart (Monthly)

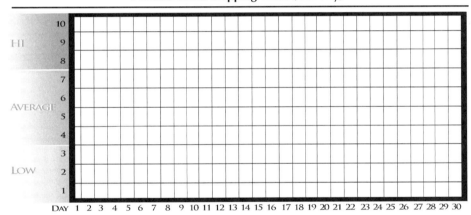

Give yourself 1 point for low score and 10 points for a high score.

All of the characteristics for the best possible Shining parenting profile are discussed in the previous chapters of this book. After carefully reading the chapters, you can, by honest evaluation, build your personal shine profile by giving yourself one point in the areas in which you reach the best shine.   Add up your total score and place on Profile Shine Chart daily for a monthly glance at how well you are bringing home the shine! You can color your bar graphs for a better view.

- Parenting Style:
- Time Manager by having him work a talent one hour a day … in segments or whole
- Discipline System… Train by example; teach character and discipline with respect and consequences.
- Shine Character. Building Bee-lieving character traits; I am better than a bumblebee I can fly
- Using my personal shine Profile to keep me flying

- Staying on track of Big Picture
- Nurturing Healthy Self
- Nurturing healthy relationships attachments, bonding, - up communication
- Personality Style using your best strengths
- Communication style; active listening
- Using up words and filling love tanks

A
P
P
E
N
D
I
X

i

<u>Notes</u>

_____

_____

_____

_____

_____

_____

_____

_____

_____

_____

Pocket Full O' Stars Inc.

Calendar For Shining Star

Name_____

Shining Clay_____

Month_____

Prayer time, Bible time, feed pet, vacuum room, dust furniture, living room, family room, my room, dishes, laundry, personal grooming.

Week One	Week Two	Week Three	Week Four
Sunday reserved for Church, Family	Sunday reserved for Church, Family	Sunday reserved for Church, Family	Sunday reserved for Church, Family

Calendar displays sticker for each day "shining clay" (name) _____ , shined his/her clay responsibilities for that day.
Below write name of responsibility / time / day:

_____

(Clean sink, make bed, hang up clothes, brush teeth, groom hair etc.).
Reward System varies with individual age etc.

Weekly or more Shining stars =_____or falling stars = _____
Weekly Friday/Sat awards family night, starring star, recording on family recorder,
Gift ideas for month: Bible with name, Bible store gift certificate, new dress, new shirt, special shoes, or something that the star student is working towards.

Confrontational Skills
Cool Handles for Hot Pots

The "I" Message	-Verses-	The "You" Message

Focus on Behavior Example: I need help picking these things up now.	Focus on Child Example: You sure made a mess
Explains why behavior is not acceptable Example: I do not like it when I see mud on the floor.	Blames the Child Example: You ought to be ashamed.
Invites cooperation Example: I cannot hear you when you scream.	Invites uncooperativeness Example: You better shut up!

"Talk so Kids will Listen and Listen so Kids will Talk"

Praise And Self Esteem
Instead of Evaluating, Describe!

• Describe what you see.
Example: I see a clean carpet, a smooth bed, and toys neatly lined up.

• Describe how this makes you feel
Example: I really like walking into this bedroom. It makes me feel happy!

Pocket Full O' Stars Inc.

A P P E N D I X i

Listening Skills Evaluation Form

Are You A Good Listener?

In the exercise below, you will find traits of good listening and common problems people face when listening. Underneath each sentence below, you will see a series of numbers. Read the statement and then truthfully rate yourself. Underline the number you think best describes you at this present time and circle the number you would one day like to be.

1.   I am a patient listener and never try to rush a speaker.
   Rarely...   1   2   3   4   5   6   7   8   9   10   ...Usually

2.   I listen without trying to be in control of a conversation.
   Rarely...   1   2   3   4   5   6   7   8   9   10   ...Usually

3.   I am comfortable with silence.
   Rarely...   1   2   3   4   5   6   7   8   9   10   ...Usually

4.   I am able to listen to a person's feelings of anger and resentment without becoming personally involved.
   Rarely...   1   2   3   4   5   6   7   8   9   10   ...Usually

5.   I am an attentive listener, rarely finding myself distracted.
   Rarely...   1   2   3   4   5   6   7   8   9   10   ...Usually

6.   I can keep things confidential
   Rarely...   1   2   3   4   5   6   7   8   9   10   ...Usually

7.   I stop what I am doing to listen to what a person is saying.
   Rarely...   1   2   3   4   5   6   7   8   9   10   ...Usually

8.   I rarely interrupt and am careful to wait for a person to finish speaking before I express my thoughts.
   Rarely...   1   2   3   4   5   6   7   8   9   10   ...Usually

9.   I am empathetic.
   Rarely...   1   2   3   4   5   6   7   8   9   10   ...Usually

10.   I am tolerant and try not to be critical of what a person is saying.
   Rarely...   1   2   3   4   5   6   7   8   9   10   ...Usually

Time Manager for Daily Shine

6:00 _____

7:00 _____

8:00 _____

9:00 _____

10:00 _____

11:00 _____

12:00 _____

1:00 _____

2:00 _____

3:00 _____

4:00 _____

5:00 _____

6:00 _____

7:00 _____

8:00 _____

9:00 _____

10:00 _____

A P P E N D I X i

Jobs for Your Children
Children Like to Help

Responsibility is the best teacher. By giving them small responsibilities when they are young and larger responsibilities as they grow older, you are training them to one day become responsible adults. Since home is the training ground for life, it is only right that everyone becomes enlisted! You are the greatest and most important teacher your child will ever know. Teach your child how to complete his or her assigned job. When he or she has completed the job well, fill them with positive statements. This will in turn make them have a positive attitude towards their jobs. Teach your children to be hard workers, and this quality will never leave them as they continue their journey of life.

3 to 4 years old
1.   Brush teeth
2.   Get dressed, put pajamas away
3.   Help empty dishwasher
4.   Empty waste basket
5.   Put away toys

5 to 6 years old
1.   Clean bathroom sinks
2.   Clean up after pet
3.   Help set table
4.   Vacuum
5.   Help clean and straighten bedroom

7 to 8 years old
1.   Dry dishes
2.   Kitchen helper
3.   Piano Lessons
4.   Help make lunches for school
5.   Empty garbage

9 to 10 years old
1.   Polish shoes
2.   Learn to play an instrument
3.   Wash windows
4.   Help wash car
5.   Clean entire bathroom

Shining Star Chart

Weekly Chart	☆	☾	☺	♡	☀	♡	⌒
Morning Shine	Mon.	Tues.	Wed.	Thurs.	Fri.	Sat.	Sun
Wake up Smile							
Make Bed							
Eat Breakfast							
Brush Teeth							
Get Dressed							
Noon Shine							
Cheery Smile							
Eat Lunch							
Pick up Toys							
Be Kind							
Be Honest							
Evening Shine							
Cheery Smile							
Eat Dinner							
Brush Teeth							
Pick up Toys							
Bath							
Put away clothes							
Say prayers & Bible time							
Cheery goodnight							

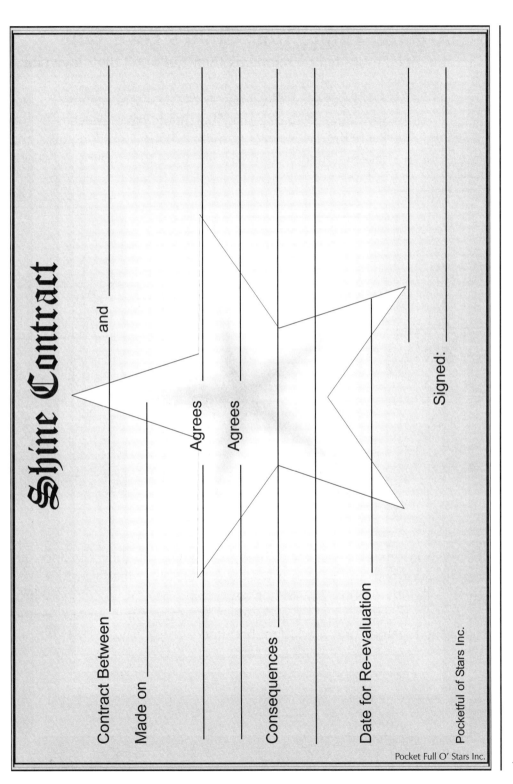

Shine Contract

Contract Between _____ and _____

Made on _____

_____ Agrees _____

_____ Agrees _____

Consequences _____

Date for Re-evaluation _____

Signed: _____

Pocketful of Stars Inc.

Pocket Full O' Stars Inc.

Are You Filling Your Child's Love Tank?
Children need more happy moments than sad to fill their love tank.

Choose five of the ideas below every day. Every time you accomplish one idea, fill the happy basket with one star. You should have five stars by the end of the day. Every time you forget to make a happy moment, take one star out of the basket. The next day you will have to double your efforts to fill your child's love tank. (You can have your children do this, also)

Give a hug, smile at your child, hold their hand, rub their shoulder, sit on the floor with them, take a walk together, say "Hello sunshine" as they walk into a room, play Simon says, color a picture together, share quiet time together, take a nap together, hold them in your lap, sing a silly song together, and read them bedtime stories. Say, "I love you."

APPENDIX i

A Place To Shine

150 Areas Your Child Can Shine

I would like to personally suggest the A.C.T.S. (Association of Christian Teachers and Schools) Convention Center as a particular outstanding place for your child to partcipate. It is a golden door of opportunity awaiting to be explored with over 150 entries. This convention gives every child a chance to shine somewhere. I was overwhelmed at the participation and beautiful camp setting. Ribbons, trophies, and accolades of praise are awarded students in a first class manner. I have provided a list of the entries below with permission from Bro. Batchelor, director of the A.C.T.S. The A.C.T.S. convention center has a wide spectrum of students who are qualified to attend from home-schoolers, Christian academies, and public schools. Contact information: 302-424-4652

As a parent, it is our responsibility to constantly seek ways our children can be involved and assist in every possible way to make it a reality. Helping your child to be involved may mean trips to an event or it may mean providing extra funds for traveling in groups. This may not be convenient, but on the other hand, if you want to provide your child with these "Shining" moments, the hard work is worth it. Considering the negative outcomes that some parents pay in bails and other heart-breaking situations, the price for landing a positive shine is very affordable.

Academic Division
General
Bible Memory
Checkers
Chess
Spelling
History
Science-Collection
Science-Research
Science-Engineering
Science-Theoretical
Team
Creative Composition
Essay Writing
Poetry Writing
Short Story Writing
Web Site Design
Power Point
Presentation
Christian Service
Soul Winning Award
Golden Apple Award
Golden Lamb Award
Golden Harp Award
Christian Soldier Award
Art Division
Brush/Pen/Knife
Oil
Watercolor
Acrylic
Sketching
nd Ink
Colored Pencils
Pastels
Tools
(M/F) Woodwork
(M) Clay Sculpture
(M) Metal Working
Photography Division
Black and White
Character Portrait
Scenic
Still Life
Wild Life
Photo Journalism
Character Trait Picture
Color
Character Portrait
Scenic
Still Life
Wild Life
Special Effects
Character
Trait Picture
Needle/Thread Division
Garments
Sportswear
Dresses
Formals
Coats
Coordinates

Needlecraft
Counted Cross-Stitch
Embroidery
Crewel
Needle Point
Crochet
 Knitting
Quilts
Afghans
Athletic Division
Male
Track
100-Meter Dash
200-Meter Dash
400-Meter Dash
800-Meter Dash
1600-Meter Dash
400-Meter Relay
1600-Meter Relay
Field Events
High Jump
Running Long Jump
Shot-Put
Discus
Soccer Kick
Pentathlon
Physical Fitness
Basketball
Table Tennis (Singles)
Tennis (Single)
Archery
Unlimited Free Style
Bare Compound Bow
Traditional Instinctive
Athletic Division
Female
Track
100-Meter Dash
200-Meter Dash
400-Meter Dash
800-Meter Dash
1600-Meter Dash
400-Meter Relay
1600-Meter Relay
Archery
Unlimited Free Style
Bare Compound Bow
Traditional Instinctive
Table Tennis (Singles)
Tennis (Single)
Volleyball
Drill Team Color
Guard/Fag Corps
Drill Team (M)
Color Guard (M)
Flag Corps (F)
Music Division
Small Vocal
Male solo
Female solo
Male Duet
Female Duet

Mixed Duet
Large Vocal
Male Trio
Female Trio
Mixed Trio
Male Quartet
Female Quartet
Small Ensemble
Large Ensemble
Choir
Instrumental Division
Solo- Piano (Male)
Solo-Piano (Female)
Solo-Woodwind
Solo- String (Plucked)
Solo – String (Bowed)
Solo- Brass
Solo-Miscellaneous
Duet- Piano
Duet-Instrumental
Quartet-Instrumental
Sm. Instr. Ensemble
Lg. Instr. Ensemble
Handbell Choir
Music Composition
Persuasive/ Dramatic Division
(Male- Female)
Oratory (F)
Oral Argument(M-F)
Dramatic Monoloque (F)
Expressive Reading (M)
Famous Speech (M)
Poetry Recitation (M-F)
Dramatic Dialogue (M-F)
Preaching (M)
Clown Act (M-F)
One-Act Play
Illus. Storytelling (M-F)
Puppets(M-F)
Inter. For Deaf (M-F)
Radio program
Entry
Scripture Video

A.T.C.S. Convention Entries.
Used with permision

APPENDIX ii
ACKNOWLEDGEMENTS AND BIBLIOGRAPHY

The Andrus Family

Top row: Cherie' and Greg Makosky - Joel, Angela, and Shiloh Andrus
Bottom row: Gregory and Garrison Makosky - Royce and Glenda Andrus

Royce and Glenda live about twenty-five minutes from the Atlantic Ocean, in Milford, Delaware. Here they have given their lives to the area and the dear people of their hearts, Lighthouse Christian Center. Their lives have been blessed by their children starting with the youngest, their son Joel, Angela, Shiloh, Cherie', and son-in-law Greg Makosky. Precious moments are the ones shared with their two grandsons: Gregory 4 and Garrison 18 months. Glenda has a B.S. from Delaware State University in early childhood education and has served as the director of Lighthouse Christian Academy for over twenty-five years. Glenda has had the honor of serving on the Early Education Task Board for Delaware's Governor, Ruth Ann Minner. Presently, she serves as a parenting instructor for Child Inc. and also as a parenting motivational speaker.

Contact Information:
19 the Mead
Houston, Delaware 19954
lccmilford@aol.com
302-424-4652 or 302-422-7047

Acknowledgments

Cover & Layout Design: Angela Andrus
Editor and Illustrator: Shiloh Andrus

To The Staff of Classic Publishing Company:
Editors: Lisa Taylor and Barbara Vecore
Executive Manager: Diana Gillespie
Executive Director: Pastor Janet Trout - To my former superintendent, Pastor Wayne Trout. My Aunt & Uncle, heroes always

Complimentary-Gifted people: Thank you for surrounding me with your time, talent, and energy. Thank you for helping me bring this dream to birth. You are the best.

To Lighthouse Christian Center, Academy staff, and friends: You are my forever family, my support and prayer partners for the sake of the cause.

To my friends and mentors: Thank you for investing so much into the lives of my children, Royce and myself.

To my husband's family: My love to you. You are close in our hearts always.

To my personal family: We painted the picture of life together as kids. How beautiful each color was. Each reflected the wonderful loving memories we share. Thank you for loving me through all of them. Without your love, I could not paint anymore.

To my precious children: You are the greatest gifts and stars God has ever given me.   Shiloh, Angela, Joel, Cherie, and Greg
To my grandchildren Gregory & Garrison. You are my little shining stars.

To my husband, Royce: You are my all time hero, my mainline supporter and the forever love of my lifetime. I could never thank you enough for your love, inspiration, and your heart of velvet steel that has kept our home focused clear upon "The Big Picture".   Love is Forever, Glenda

To Jesus Christ, my Morning Star, the Rock and Anchor that holds our hearts and homes together. Thank You for helping me write this project. Without You there would be no need of writing.

Bibliography

Chapman, Gary. (1995). *The Five Love Languages: How to Express Heartfelt Commitment to Your Mate.* Chicago: Northfield Publishing.

Curie, Marie. Sklodowska. (January 1904). Discovery of Radium. *Century Magazine.* American Institute of Physics.

Dobson, James. (2001). *Bringing Up Boys.* Wheaton, IL: Tyndale House Publishers.

Dobson, James. (1997). *Parenting Isn't for Cowards.* New York: Inspirational Press.

Dobson, James. (1997). *The Strong-Willed Child.* New York: Inspirational Press.

Elmore, Tim. (2001). *Nurturing the Leader Within Your Child.* Nashville, TN: Thomas Nelson Publishers.

Forster, Pam. (1995). *Plants Grow Up.* Oregon: Doorposts.

Fagan, P. F. (March 17, 1995). The Real Root Cause of Violent Crime: The Breakdown of Marriage, Family, and Community. *Backgrounder #1026.* The Heritage Foundation.

Fagan, P. F. and Hanks, D. B. (June 3, 1997). Social Scientific Data on the Impact of Marriage and Divorce on Children. Backgrounder #1115. The Heritage Foundation.

Guarendi, Ray. (2003). *Discipline That Lasts a Lifetime: The Best Gift You Can Give Your Kids.* Ann Arbor, MI: Servant Publications.

Holy Bible. King James Version.

Inrig, Elizabeth. (2001). *Release Your Potential: Using Your Gifts in a Thriving Women's Ministry.* Chicago: Moody Press.

Lahaye, Beverly. *Understanding Your Child's Temperment.* Eugene, Oregon: Harvest House Publishers.

Leman, Kevin. (2000). *Making Children Mind Without Losing Yours.* Grand Rapids, MI: Fleming H. Revell.

Literaurer, Florence. (1992) *Personality Plus.* Tarrytown, New York: Fleming H. Revel Company.

Mandino, Og. (1992). *The Return of the Ragpicker.* United States: Bantam.

McGraw, Phil. (2004). *Family First: Your Step-by-Step Plan for Creating a Phenomenal Family.* New York: Free Press.

Sears, William and Sears, Marsha. (2002) *The Successful Child.* New York: Little, Brown and Co.

Tobias, Cynthia Ulrich. (1996). *Every Child Can Succeed: Making the Most of Your Child's Learning Style.* Wheaton, IL: Tyndale House Publishers.

Ziglar, Zig. (1978). *See You at the Top.* Louisiana: Pelican Publishing Company, Inc.

APPENDIX ii

NOTES

Notes

NOTES

Notes

NOTES

NOTES

NOTES